This is a unique, helpful and enjoyable guide to the book of Acts. Key teaching by Kevin DeYoung is provided in an accessible and compelling way. This will be a wonderful introduction and refresher for those wanting an overview of the book of Acts.

Sam Allberry

Apologist, RZIM; author of *Why Bother With Church?* and *Is God Anti-Gay?*

What communication! As a dyslexic I love pictures and I found the combination of images and texts took the Books of Acts from black and white to colour. In fact I think my mind has now almost photographed some of the pages. I was particularly gripped by the references to other parts of the Bible, which gloriously filled out the story of Acts.

Rico Tice

Co-author of Christianity Explored
& Associate Minister at All Souls Church, London

The Word of God is living and active, beautiful and poetic. It should touch the senses. I love what Kevin and Chris have done here. The truth of God's word is beautifully presented in a way that informs the head while stirring the heart.

Matt Chandler

Lead Pastor of The Village Church, Flower Mound, Texas

Someone has said, that the human brain is much more a picture gallery than a debating hall! That being the case this visual depiction of Acts is perfect for us as we remember far more readily what we see than what we hear. Kevin DeYoung and Chris Ranson have produced a wonderfully creative and Biblically faithful visual commentary on Acts, hopefully the first of many.

David Cook

Former Principal and Director of the School of Preaching
at Sydney Missionary and Bible College, Sydney, Australia

An incredibly enlightening and inspiring presentation of one of the most significant eras of human history! I am amazed at how Kevin's trademark theological precision has been put into such an engaging format. I am not sure who will get more out of it—kids, teens or adults! I am excited to use this with my own family.

J.D. Greear

Pastor of The Summit Church, Raleigh-Durham, North Carolina

To Morag

ACTS

A VISUAL GUIDE

KEVIN DEYOUNG
& CHRIS RANSON

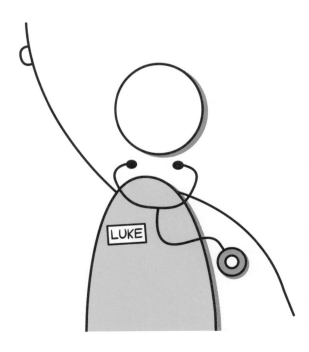

Copyright © Chris Ranson and Kevin DeYoung, 2018

ISBN 978-1-5271-0139-5

10 9 8 7 6 5 4 3 2 1

Published in 2018
by
Christian Focus Publications Ltd,
Geanies House, Fearn,
Ross-shire, IV20 1TW, Scotland.
www.christianfocus.com

Cover design by MOOSE77

Illustrated by Chris Ranson

Printed by Bell and Bain, Glasgow.

HOW TO USE THIS BOOK

This book is a Visual Guide to the Bible book of Acts. As such, the only way to read it is to have Acts open in front of you. You may want to follow the steps outlined below each time you pick it up:

1. Pray. Remember, reading the Bible (even with a Visual Guide) is not like reading any other book. Pray that the Holy Spirit would help you understand and apply what you read (John 14:26; 16:13).

2. Read the relevant passage from Acts first. This is highlighted in yellow at the top of each section in the Visual Guide.

3. Make your way through the guide, ensuring that you understand what is being said in the Bible. Take time to ask yourself the questions that come up in the Visual Guide and prayerfully consider any points of application.

4. If you would like to listen to Kevin DeYoung's sermons on these passages, find the links on our website: **avisualguide.com**

INTRODUCTION

I've never been good at drawing things. I learned how to master the 3D cube and Christmas trees, but that's about it. As an inveterate grade-monger, I was thankful that my high school art class gave good marks for working hard and showing improvement. I barely know how to color.

So it's without exaggeration that I can say I'm amazed at what Chris Ranson can do. You probably don't know of Chris. I just met him a couple of years go. But what he does is impressive. While working as an engineer and a designer, this native of Scotland was introduced to the world of visual note taking. One Sunday, after years of regular sermon notes, Chris decided to try *drawing* (instead of writing) what the preacher was saying. At first, the sketches were pretty plain, but over time Chris found out he was quite good at this new form of note taking, and he made the mental switch to thinking in pictures. The fruit of Chris' gifts and hard work is what you're holding in your hand.

At the beginning of 2016 I traveled to Scotland to preach a series of messages in Edinburgh. Unbeknownst to me, Chris was there listening. He discovered that my sermons—I suppose, with their orderly Presbyterian structure and clear points and sub-points—worked especially well with his kind of note taking. A few weeks later, I was contacted by Christian Focus with some crazy idea about a Scottish guy who wanted to listen to two years' worth of my sermons and draw pictures. I didn't know what to expect, but I thought, 'Hey, why not?'

The project has exceeded my expectations. Chris is not only a gifted artist, he's a student of the Bible and a careful listener of preaching. I'm eager to see what the Lord might do with this book—to inspire a fresh way of taking notes, to put sermons in front of people who might otherwise be disinterested, or simply to get people into the book of Acts.

I'm grateful to Christian Focus for using my sermons as a part of this unique project. I pray that God would be glorified and the church edified as Christians (and non-Christians!) work their way through these messages and Chris' notes. In listening to the sermons while using the visual notes, you may just find that even if a picture is worth a thousand words, sometimes you don't have to choose between the two.

Kevin DeYoung

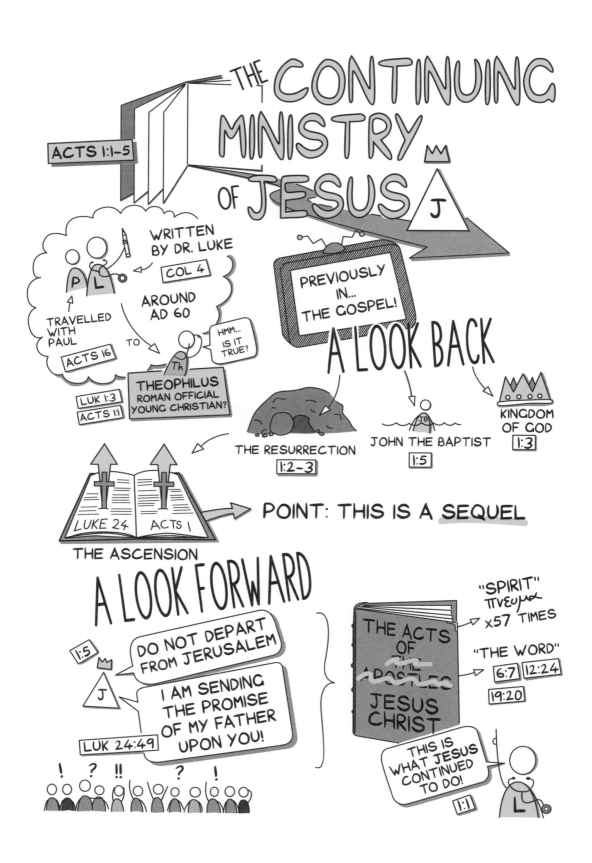

ACTS

...IS THE STORY OF THE **CONTINUING WORK** OF JESUS

WHAT DIFFERENCE DOES THAT MAKE?

① THERE ARE MORE CHAPTERS TO THE GOSPEL

- ○ HIS WORK
- ○ HIS DEATH
- ○ HIS RESURRECTION
- ○ HIS SESSION
- ○ PENTECOST

THE FORGOTTEN CHAPTER!

② THIS IS **JESUS'** MINISTRY

MATT 16:18

IT IS **JESUS** WHO BUILDS THE CHURCH

YOU ARE **NOT** THE STAR OF THE SHOW

③ NOTHING IS POSSIBLE WITHOUT JESUS

EVEN IF YOUR CHURCH IS SUPER-ACTIVE!

AND GREAT THINGS ARE POSSIBLE WITH JESUS

JOHN 15:5

THE SPIRIT OF GOD AND THE WORD OF GOD ARE MORE THAN ENOUGH TO DO THE WORK OF GOD

AS LONG AS JESUS MINISTERS, WE CAN TOO

UP AND AWAY

ACTS 1:6-11

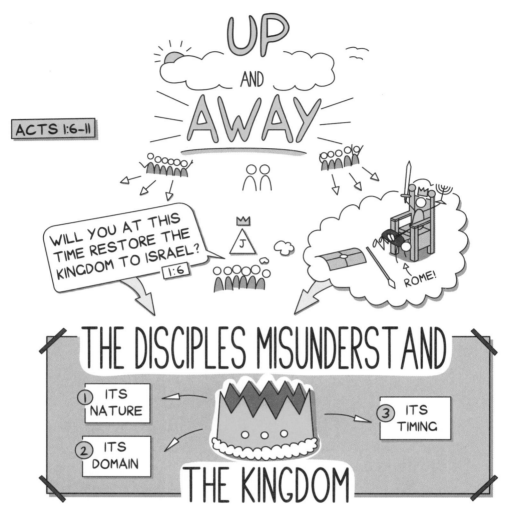

WILL YOU AT THIS TIME RESTORE THE KINGDOM TO ISRAEL? 1:6

ROME!

THE DISCIPLES MISUNDERSTAND

1. ITS NATURE
2. ITS DOMAIN
3. ITS TIMING

THE KINGDOM

1. THE KINGDOM IS HEAVENLY AND SPIRITUAL

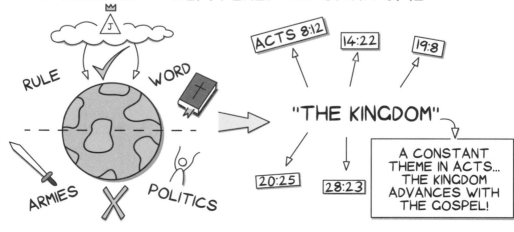

RULE

WORD

ARMIES

POLITICS

ACTS 8:12   14:22   19:8

"THE KINGDOM"

20:25   28:23

A CONSTANT THEME IN ACTS... THE KINGDOM ADVANCES WITH THE GOSPEL!

② THE KINGDOM IS UNIVERSAL... NOT NATIONAL

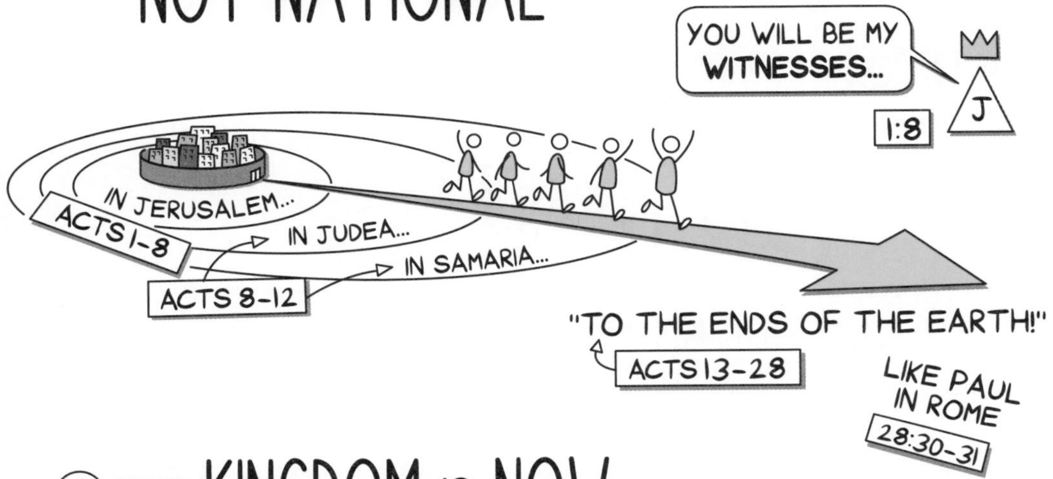

YOU WILL BE MY WITNESSES...

1:8

IN JERUSALEM...

ACTS 1-8

IN JUDEA...

IN SAMARIA...

ACTS 8-12

"TO THE ENDS OF THE EARTH!"

ACTS 13-28

LIKE PAUL IN ROME

28:30-31

③ THE KINGDOM IS NOW... AND NOT YET

STOP LOOKING UP! (YOU HAVE A JOB TO DO!)

1:1

"YOU WILL RECEIVE POWER"

1:8

THE COMMAND: 1:8

THIS IS THE JESUS I KNOW

PRO JESUS!

DON'T JUST BE AN ADVOCATE...

BE A WITNESS!

DO THIS IN CONFIDENCE

BECAUSE THE **HOLY SPIRIT** EMPOWERS YOU

ACTS 2:17   4:31   6:8

GETTING THE BAND BACK TOGETHER

ACTS 1:12-26

YOU WILL BE MY WITNESSES
1:8

WHY BOTHER TELLING US THIS?

Matthias chosen...

1:12-26

GOD'S PLAN IS INDESTRUCTIBLE

THE WICKED WILL BE JUDGED

1:15

THIS IS WHAT HAPPENED TO WICKED JUDAS

Pe

PETER

120 FOLLOWERS

WAITING (OBEDIENTLY)
LUKE 24:49

ALL PRAYING
ACTS 1:14

NO JUDAS?

1:16-19

GOD WILL NOT BE MOCKED
ACTS 5:5   12:23

REMEMBER

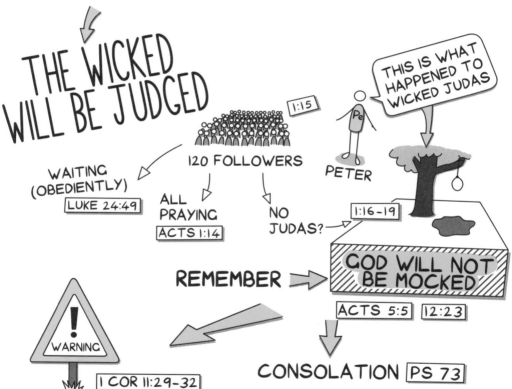

WARNING

1 COR 11:29-32

CONSOLATION   PS 73

GOD CAN JUDGE SINNERS TODAY

→ INSTANTLY

GOD (NOT YOU) WILL PUNISH YOUR ENEMIES

THE SCRIPTURES WILL BE FULFILLED

THIS HAD TO HAPPEN 1:16

PS 69:25 | 109:8

JUDAS WAS GOD'S PLAN

EVEN IN THE **DARKEST** TIMES, GOD IS WORKING FOR YOUR <u>GOOD</u>

GOD WILL HAVE HIS WITNESSES

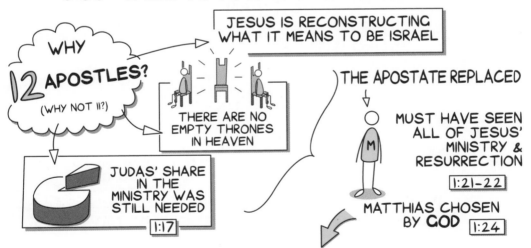

JESUS IS RECONSTRUCTING WHAT IT MEANS TO BE ISRAEL

WHY 12 APOSTLES? (WHY NOT 11?)

THERE ARE NO EMPTY THRONES IN HEAVEN

JUDAS' SHARE IN THE MINISTRY WAS STILL NEEDED 1:17

THE APOSTATE REPLACED

MUST HAVE SEEN ALL OF JESUS' MINISTRY & RESURRECTION 1:21-22

MATTHIAS CHOSEN BY **GOD** 1:24

NO MATTER WHAT HAPPENS
OUR GOD WILL HAVE HIS WAY

THIS NEW DAY MEANS...

WARNING → GOD'S JUDGMENT COMES SOON

HOPE → CHRIST RULES FROM HIS THRONE

A NEW EXPERIENCE

OLD TESTAMENT

ONLY CERTAIN INDIVIDUALS RECEIVED THE HOLY SPIRIT
E.G. NUM 11:24-30

1:17-18

NOW GOD'S SPIRIT IS POURED OUT ON **ALL** GOD'S PEOPLE
← A GOSPEL HARVEST

AN OLD MESSAGE WITH A NEW TWIST

EVERYONE WHO CALLS UPON THE **NAME** OF THE LORD WILL BE SAVED
(OLD MESSAGE)

THE 'NAME' IS **JESUS** ACTS 4:12
(THAT'S NEW!)

THE INVITATION IS **GLOBAL**

GOSPEL

THIS Ⓙ JESUS

THE CENTERPOINT OF THE CHRISTIAN FAITH

ACTS 2:22-28

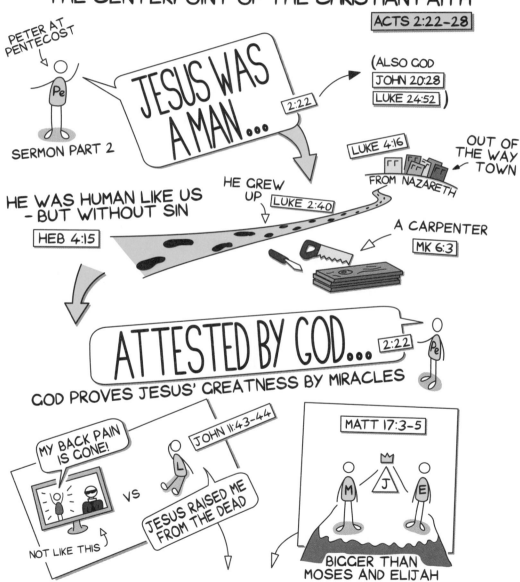

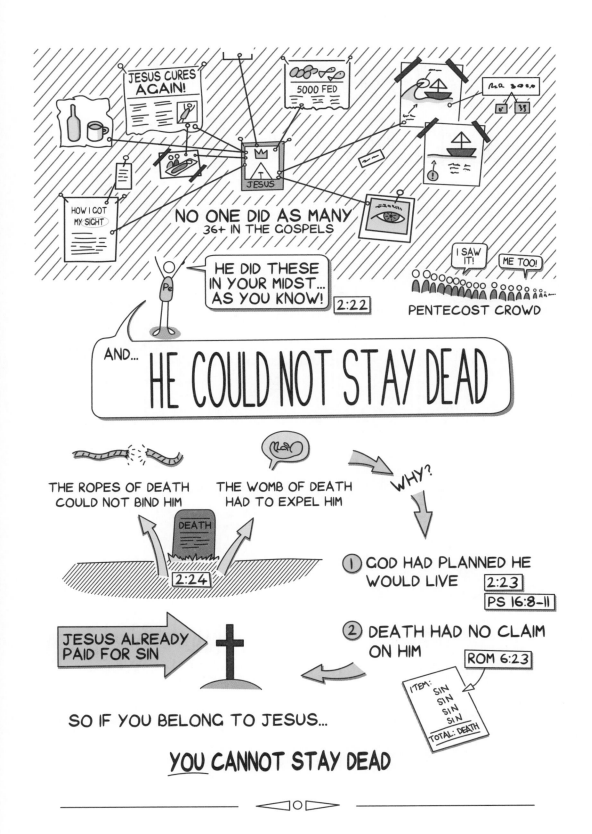

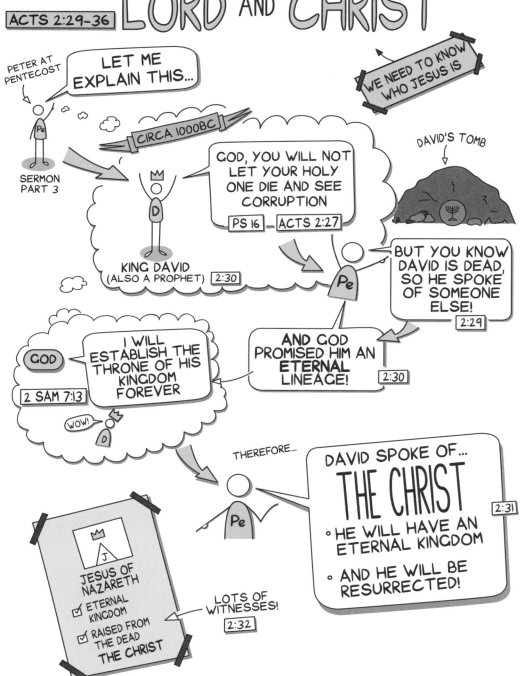

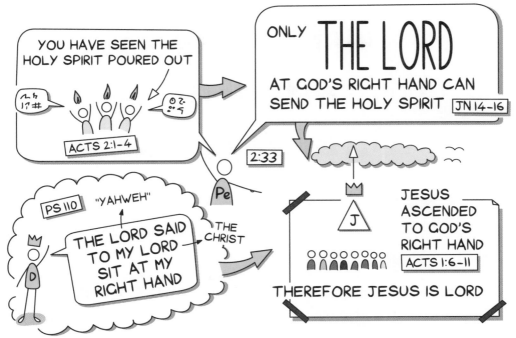

YOU HAVE SEEN THE HOLY SPIRIT POURED OUT

ACTS 2:1-4

ONLY **THE LORD** AT GOD'S RIGHT HAND CAN SEND THE HOLY SPIRIT JN 14-16

2:33

Pe

JESUS ASCENDED TO GOD'S RIGHT HAND ACTS 1:6-11

THEREFORE JESUS IS LORD

PS 110 "YAHWEH"

THE LORD SAID TO MY LORD SIT AT MY RIGHT HAND

THE CHRIST

D

THEREFORE KNOW FOR CERTAIN JESUS IS LORD AND CHRIST 2:36

THIS MEANS

RECOGNIZING YOU ARE A SINNER WHO NEEDS A CHRIST TO SAVE YOU...

BELIEVING THE EYEWITNESS TESTIMONY THAT JESUS DIED AND ROSE FROM THE DEAD...

GIVING YOUR WHOLE LIFE TO SERVE THE TRUE LORD WHO DEMANDS AND DESERVES YOUR SERVICE

"WHAT SHALL WE DO?!"

ACTS 2:37-41

THEY WERE CUT TO THE HEART | 2:37

THIS MEANS

"WHAT YOU SAID ABOUT **US** IS TRUE – WE ARE SINNERS WHO KILLED THE CHRIST" | 2:36

"WHAT YOU SAID ABOUT **JESUS** IS TRUE – HE IS LORD AND CHRIST" | 2:36

TODAY, GOD IS CHANGING HEARTS THE SAME WAY

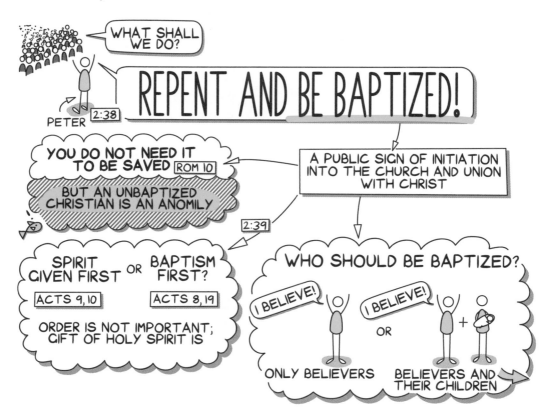

WHAT SHALL WE DO?

PETER | 2:38

REPENT AND BE BAPTIZED!

YOU DO NOT NEED IT TO BE SAVED | ROM 10

BUT AN UNBAPTIZED CHRISTIAN IS AN ANOMLY

A PUBLIC SIGN OF INITIATION INTO THE CHURCH AND UNION WITH CHRIST

| 2:39

SPIRIT GIVEN FIRST OR BAPTISM FIRST?

ACTS 9,10   ACTS 8,19

ORDER IS NOT IMPORTANT; GIFT OF HOLY SPIRIT IS

WHO SHOULD BE BAPTIZED?

I BELIEVE!   I BELIEVE!

OR

ONLY BELIEVERS   BELIEVERS AND THEIR CHILDREN

BUT REPENTANCE IS PRECIOUS TO GOD AND
NECESSARY FOR SALVATION

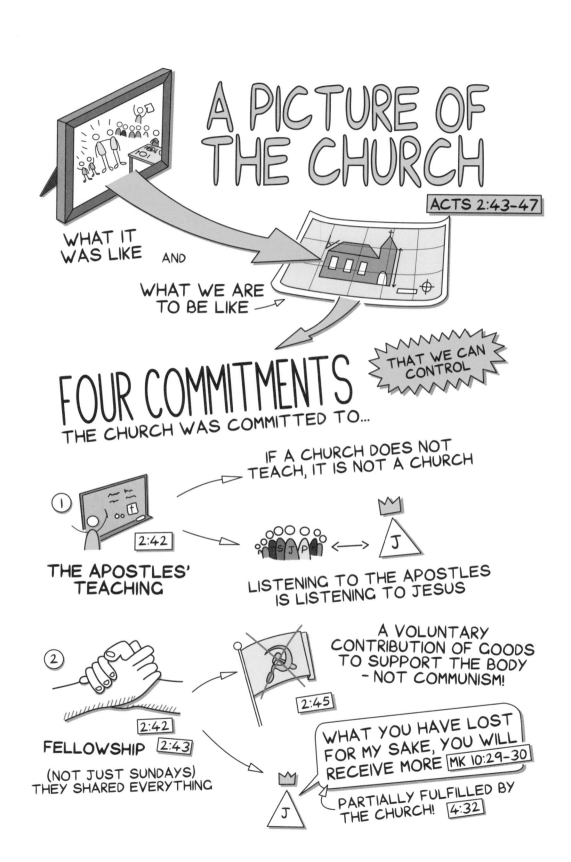

③

BREAKING BREAD
`2:42`

THE LORD'S
SUPPER
`20:7`

SHARED
MEAL
`2:46`

④

PRAYER `2:42`

SET PRAYERS (SEE `3:1`)
WE CAN USE SCRIPTURE,
HYMNS AND BOOKS TO
HELP US PRAY!

INFORMAL
PRAYER

DEMONSTRATES
DEPENDENCE ON GOD

THESE ARE THE
FOUR PARTS OF
REGULAR WORSHIP

CHECK
OUT →

JUSTIN MARTYR

FIRST
APOLOGY

(CHAP 67)
AD 155

THREE RESULTS

THAT WE CAN'T
CONTROL

FEAR `2:43`

BECAUSE OF SIGNS
AND WONDERS

AND BECAUSE THE
CHURCH WAS A
PEOPLE WHO TOOK
GOD **SERIOUSLY**

FAITH `2:47`

NEW CONVERTS
DAILY

FAVOR
`2:47`

WOW THOSE
CHRISTIANS
ARE REALLY
LOVING

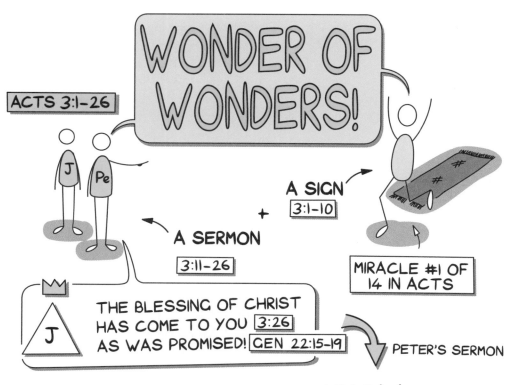

WONDER OF WONDERS!

ACTS 3:1-26

A SIGN
3:1-10

MIRACLE #1 OF 14 IN ACTS

A SERMON
3:11-26

THE BLESSING OF CHRIST HAS COME TO YOU 3:26 AS WAS PROMISED! GEN 22:15-19

PETER'S SERMON

GOD WANTS YOU TO KNOW YOUR PRIVILEGE...

3:13-15

3:16

THEY WERE EYE-WITNESSES TO JESUS' DEATH, RESURRECTION AND TO THIS MIRACLE!

YOU LIKELY HAVE ACCESS TO NUMEROUS CHURCHES, CHRISTIAN BOOKS, THE BIBLE, PEOPLE PRAYING FOR YOU...

YOUR SIN...

THEY DELIVERED JESUS TO THE ROMANS `3:13`

YOU MAY WANT THINGS MORE THAN JESUS...

NOTE: IGNORANCE IS NOT AN EXCUSE! `3:17-19`

YOUR SAVIOR...

MAN

GOD

- HE IS A FALSE PROPHET `JOHN 8:52`

- HE IS A BLASPHEMER `LUKE 5:21`

- MAN GAVE LIFE TO A MURDERER `3:14`

- MAN DENIED HIM BEFORE PILATE `3:13`

- MAN WOULD NOT SAVE HIM

HUGE CHASM OF THOUGHT!

- HE IS THE PROPHET `3:22`

- HE IS THE HOLY ONE OF ISRAEL `3:14`

- GOD SAID THEY MURDERED THE AUTHOR OF LIFE `3:15`

- GOD GLORIFIED HIM IN HEAVEN `JN 17:1`

- GOD SENT HIM TO BE YOUR SAVIOR

THE FAVOR OF GOD'S BLESSING `3:19-21`

  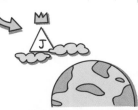

THROUGH YOUR SINS BEING BLOTTED OUT `3:19`

THROUGH SPIRITUAL REFRESHMENT `3:20`

THROUGH CHRIST'S RETURN `3:20`

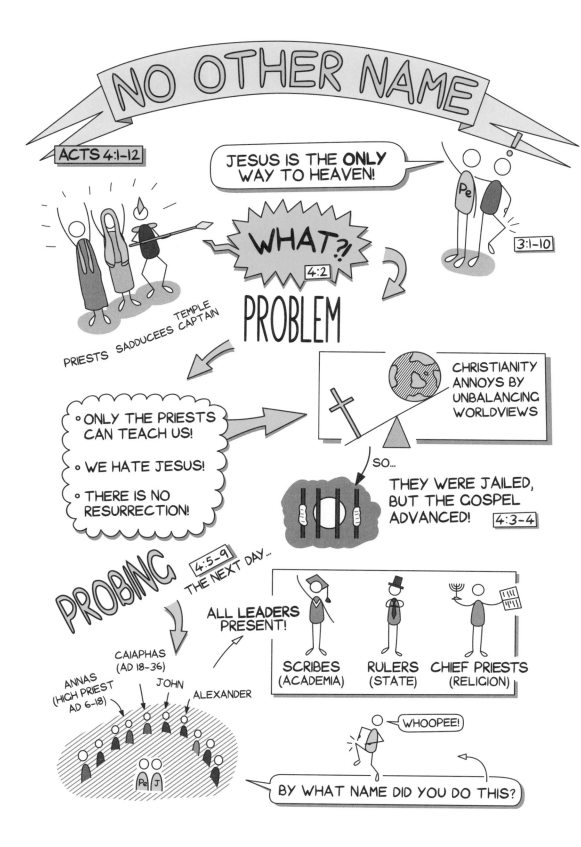

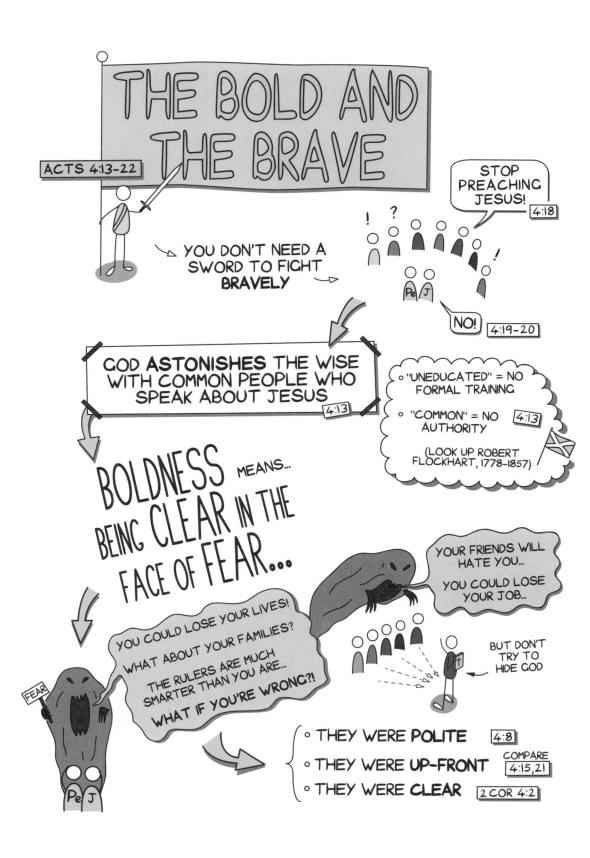

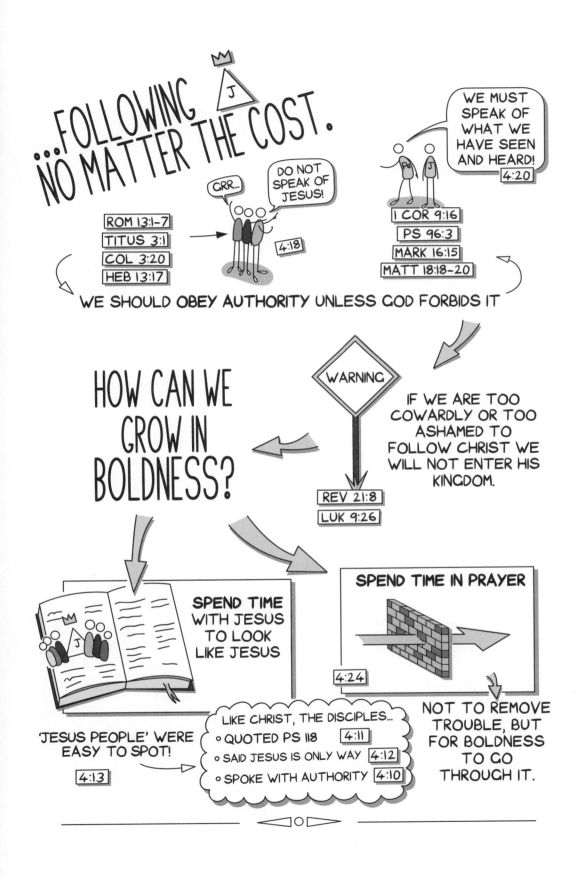

PREDESTINED GOSPEL

THE SOVEREIGNTY OF GOD... ACTS 4:23-31

PETER AND JOHN RELEASED 4:21

THIS IS WHAT HAPPENED... 4:21

NATURAL REACTION

LOOK AT THEIR THREATS 4:18 AND GRANT US BOLDNESS! 4:29

SUPERNATURAL REACTION
(AMAZING: NO WHINING OR PRAYER OF RETALIATION)

PRAYER ANSWERED 4:31

NOTICE: THE PRAYER ASKING FOR BOLDNESS REVEALS WHAT THEY KNOW ABOUT GOD 4:24-30

OUR GOD IS NOT SMALL

4:24

4:24 SOVEREIGN LORD — CREATOR OF ALL THINGS

IN GREEK: "DESPOTA"

- MASTER OF A SERVANT

SERVANT DAVID 4:25

SERVANT JESUS 4:27,30

SERVANT CHRISTIANS 4:29

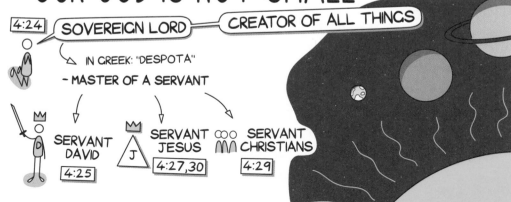

OUR GOD IS NOT SCARED

4:25-26

PS 2
- JESUS WILL BE OPPOSED
- GOD'S NOT WORRIED

GOD LAUGHS AT "THREATS"
PS 2:4

LET'S BUILD A TOWER TO HEAVEN!

GEN 11:1-9

GOD HAD TO COME DOWN JUST TO SEE THE TOWER!

OUR GOD IS NOT SURPRISED

4:27-30

WHAT CAN WE LEARN FROM GOD'S PREDESTINATION?

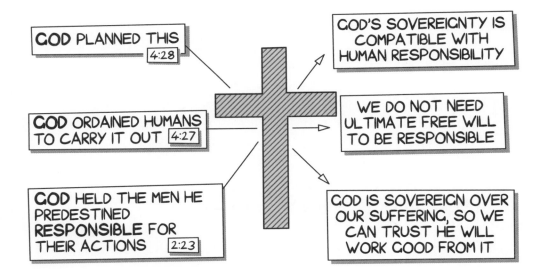

GOD PLANNED THIS
4:28

GOD ORDAINED HUMANS TO CARRY IT OUT 4:27

GOD HELD THE MEN HE PREDESTINED RESPONSIBLE FOR THEIR ACTIONS 2:23

GOD'S SOVEREIGNTY IS COMPATIBLE WITH HUMAN RESPONSIBILITY

WE DO NOT NEED ULTIMATE FREE WILL TO BE RESPONSIBLE

GOD IS SOVEREIGN OVER OUR SUFFERING, SO WE CAN TRUST HE WILL WORK GOOD FROM IT

SO... DON'T SHRINK GOD DOWN WHEN FACING TRIALS; LET HIM BE IMMEASURABLY BIG

SEE THE HEIDELBERG CATECHISM "LORD'S DAY 10" FOR MORE

Luke's gospel has the most to say about wealth & poverty. How you handle money is essential to following Christ.

THE GENEROUS GOSPEL

But he is not an evangelist against the rich but rather to the rich.

ACTS 4:32-37

"GREAT GRACE WAS UPON THEM ALL" 4:33

DEFINES THE CHURCH

THE APOSTLES' BOLD TESTIMONY
4:33

EVIDENCE OF ☑ GRACE

EVIDENCE OF ☑ GRACE

THERE WAS NO NEEDY AMONG THEM
4:34

THEY HAD EVERYTHING IN COMMON
4:32

Radical generosity

Individual ownership not state owned

(NOT COMMUNISM! PEOPLE OWNED PRIVATE PROPERTY)
4:34 5:4

"things that belong to him"

A PICTURE OF GOD'S KINGDOM ON EARTH

O.T PROMISED LAND IDEAL (SEE DT 15:4)

THE CHURCH IS GOD'S EMBASSY ON EARTH

THERE IS NO SET AMOUNT TO GIVE, BUT CHRISTIANS MUST BE GENEROUS
LK 18:18-30   LK 19:8   1 JOHN 3:16-18

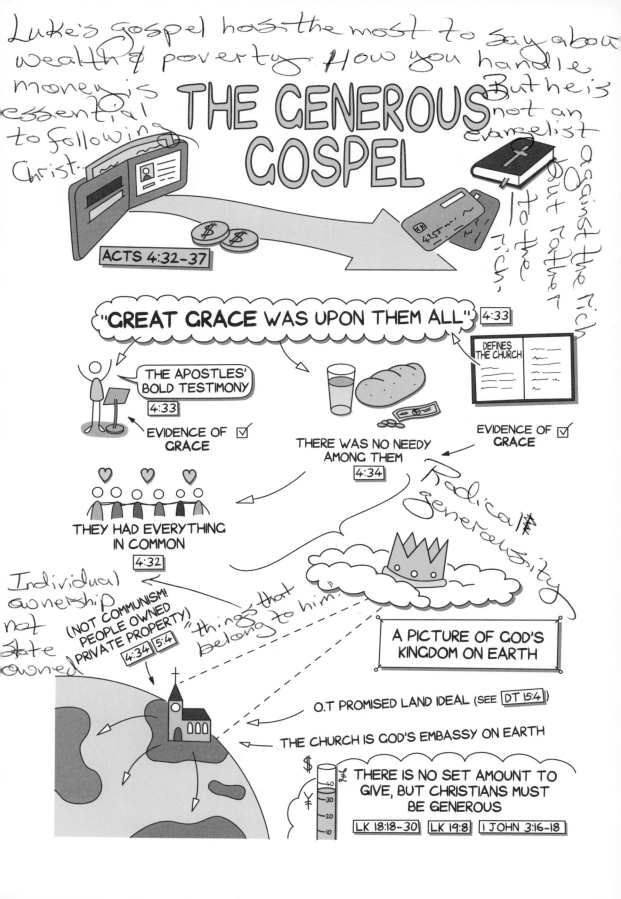

I HAVE GOT QUESTIONS!

Q. WHAT ABOUT THOSE OUTSIDE THE CHURCH?
A. "DO GOOD TO ALL, BUT ESPECIALLY TO THE HOUSEHOLD OF FAITH" GAL 6:10

Q. WHAT ABOUT THOSE SUFFERING AROUND THE WORLD?
A. EXERCISE MORAL PROXIMITY: THOSE CLOSEST TO YOU SHOULD COME FIRST, BUT NOT EXCLUSIVELY
SEE ACTS 11:27-30

Q. WON'T SOME TAKE ADVANTAGE?
A. RULES NEED TO BE ESTABLISHED TO MAKE THINGS FAIR.
ACTS 6:1-6
1 TIM 5:3-5
2 THES 3:10

LESS RESPONSIBLE
3
2
1
MOST RESPONSIBLE

1. FAMILY
2. CHURCH
3. COMMUNITY

BELIEVERS ARE OF ONE HEART AND SOUL 4:32

LIKE A MARRIAGE! (ALL THINGS SHARED)

HUMBLE
4:36-37
BARNABAS

AS A LEVITE LAND-OWNER, HE WAS WEALTHY – rich

AS A COMMITTED CHRISTIAN, HE WAS VERY GENEROUS

WOULD PEOPLE CALL YOU "SON OF ENCOURAGEMENT"?

GOOD EXAMPLE!

MONEY

TIME

HOSPITALITY, PROPERTY

FRIENDSHIP

CHILDREN

SKILLS

IF YOU ARE **RICH** IN SOMETHING, BE **GENEROUS** WITH IT

GOD HAS SHARED EVERYTHING **WITH US** SO WE CAN SHARE EVERYTHING **WITH EACH OTHER**

Model 5 Christian generousity

* Ch.5 – Bad example Ananias & Sapphira wanting to look more impressive.

I am rich. Living in a rich country.
Believe, repent, Jesus before profit, be generous, do not trust in wealth demonstrate humility.

THE UNSTOPPABLE WORD OF GOD

ACTS 5:17-42

OPPOSITION

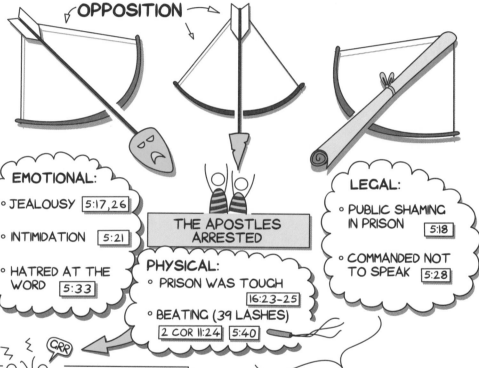

EMOTIONAL:
- JEALOUSY 5:17,26
- INTIMIDATION 5:21
- HATRED AT THE WORD 5:33

THE APOSTLES ARRESTED

PHYSICAL:
- PRISON WAS TOUGH 16:23-25
- BEATING (39 LASHES) 2 COR 11:24 5:40

LEGAL:
- PUBLIC SHAMING IN PRISON 5:18
- COMMANDED NOT TO SPEAK 5:28

GRR

THE GOSPEL HURT THE LEADERS' PRIVILEGE, POWER AND PRIDE

BUT **GOD IS WORKING** FOR THE PROGRESS OF HIS WORD

GOD WORKS BY ...

MIRACULOUS INTERVENTION

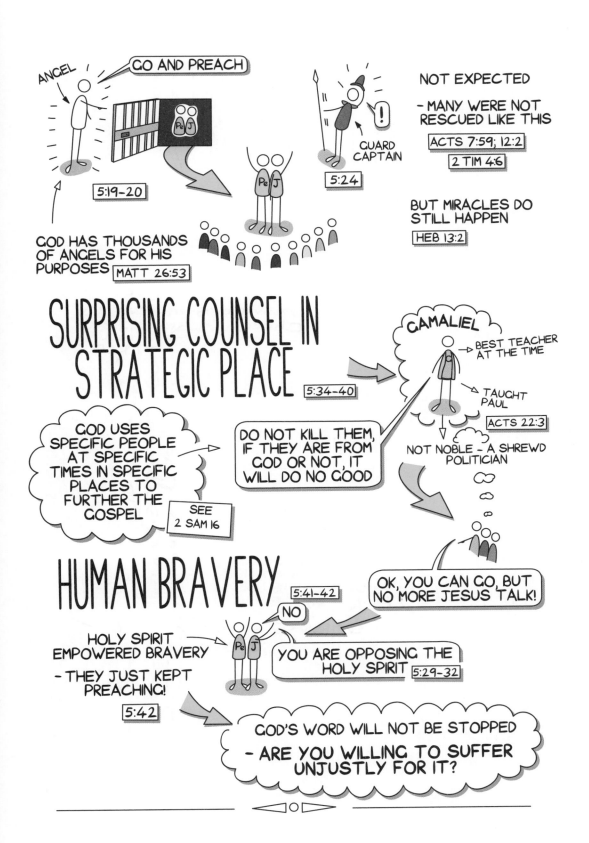

Unwise administration can unravel God's ~~words~~ Work.

ACKNOWLEDGE THE PROBLEM...

THEY HAD OPTIONS TO RESPOND...

A ☐ WE DON'T HAVE TIME TO DEAL WITH THIS!

B ☐ THAT'S NOT MY JOB!

C ☑ THE WIDOWS CAN'T WORK AND ARE STARVING... WE NEED TO SORT THIS

6:2

DELEGATE RESPONSIBILITY...

Needed spiritual men. CHOOSE 7 GODLY MEN TO SERVE 6:3

NO MICRO-MANAGING!

EMPOWERED TO MAKE CHOICE

THE APOSTLES PRAYED AND LAID HANDS ON THEM

○ WISE
○ GOOD REPUTATION
○ FILLED WITH HOLY SPIRIT
○ FROM NAMES WE CAN TELL ALL GREEK-SPEAKING 6:5

6:6

(NOT JUST A QUICK SEND OFF!)

Minorities

WISE: GREEK SPEAKERS CAN HELP THE GREEK-SPEAKING WIDOWS 6:1

...KNOW THEIR PRIORITIES

Humanitarian need
Justice concern
Prejudice?

THE RESULT 6:7

THE WORD OF GOD INCREASED

AND THE DISCIPLES MULTIPLIED

6:4 THE APOSTLES CHOSE TO **DO** SOMETHING, AND **NOT** DO SOMETHING ELSE

And back to business...

Needs do get overlooked
We do not overlook ~~offenses~~.

Good leaders know that structural problems do not need to be ignored. The goal of the church is for the Word of God to spread.

WHEN ANGELS PREPARE TO DIE

ACTS 6:8-15

STEPHEN'S STORY
(PART 1/3)

(A) INTRO 6:8-15

(B) LONG DEFENSE
(LONGEST IN ACTS)
7:1-53

(C) FIRST MARTYR
7:54-60

WHY A SPOTLIGHT
ON STEPHEN?

DR. LUKE

STEPHEN'S STORY
DISPELS TWO MYTHS:

○ "I WON'T HAVE TO FACE
WHAT JESUS FACED!"

○ "IF CALLED TO SUFFER, I
WILL BE A BAD WITNESS!"

YOU MAY HAVE TO FACE WHAT JESUS FACED

WHEN YOU SIGN
UP FOR CHRIST,
YOU SIGN UP
FOR RISK.

MATT 16:24-25

RISK

6:9

2 SYNAGOGUES
CANNOT DEFEAT
GOD-GIVEN
WISDOM 6:10

THE WORLD WILL
HATE YOU
BECAUSE OF ME
JOHN 15:18-19

J

2 TIM 3:12

BUT THE PEOPLE ARE
INCITED AGAINST
THE CHURCH
(FIRST TIME IN ACTS)

THE HISTORY OF GOD & THE REBELLION OF MAN

ACTS 6:8-15

STEPHEN'S STORY
(PART 2/3)

GRR

SPEECH MAIN FEATURES:
1. HISTORY   2. DEFENSE
3. PROSECUTION   4. HOPE

STEPHEN'S SPEECH
TO THE SANHEDRIN
(LONGEST SPEECH IN
ACTS)

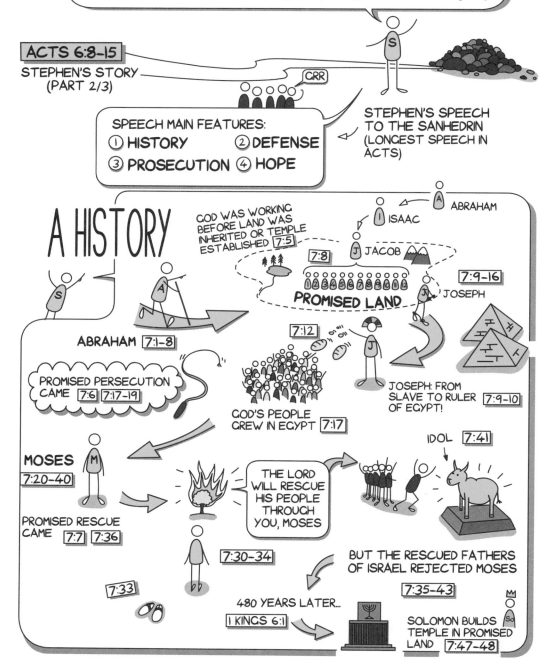

A HISTORY

GOD WAS WORKING
BEFORE LAND WAS
INHERITED OR TEMPLE
ESTABLISHED 7:5

ABRAHAM

ISAAC

7:8   JACOB

JOSEPH 7:9-16

PROMISED LAND

ABRAHAM 7:1-8

7:12

PROMISED PERSECUTION
CAME 7:6 7:17-19

GOD'S PEOPLE
GREW IN EGYPT 7:17

JOSEPH: FROM
SLAVE TO RULER
OF EGYPT! 7:9-10

MOSES
7:20-40

IDOL 7:41

THE LORD
WILL RESCUE
HIS PEOPLE
THROUGH
YOU, MOSES

PROMISED RESCUE
CAME 7:7 7:36

7:30-34

7:33

BUT THE RESCUED FATHERS
OF ISRAEL REJECTED MOSES
7:35-43

480 YEARS LATER...
1 KINGS 6:1

SOLOMON BUILDS
TEMPLE IN PROMISED
LAND 7:47-48

A CRUEL DEATH AND A HEAVENLY RECEPTION

ACTS 7:54-60

STEPHEN'S STORY
(PART 3/3)

STEPHEN'S STORY TELLS THE FAITHFUL CHRISTIAN TWO TRUTHS...

① YOU WILL HAVE ENEMIES   7:54-59

MATT 10:34-39
MATT 24:9

IN GREEK: 'THEIR HEARTS WERE CUT'... THEY WERE EXPLODING WITH ANGER!

GRINDING TEETH

THE CROWDS WERE **ENRAGED** 7:54
— NOT NORMAL ANGER

BUT WHY?

○ HE SPOKE OF **THEIR SIN**

THIS IS YOUR SINFUL HISTORY:
○ JOSEPH; YOU REJECTED
○ MOSES; YOU REJECTED
○ PROPHETS; YOU KILLED
7:9, 35, 39, 52

BUT PEOPLE LOVE THEIR SIN (STILL TRUE TODAY)

○ HE SPOKE **STRONGLY**

E.G. YOU RESIST THE HOLY SPIRIT!
7:51

J
MARK 1:22
LIKE JESUS

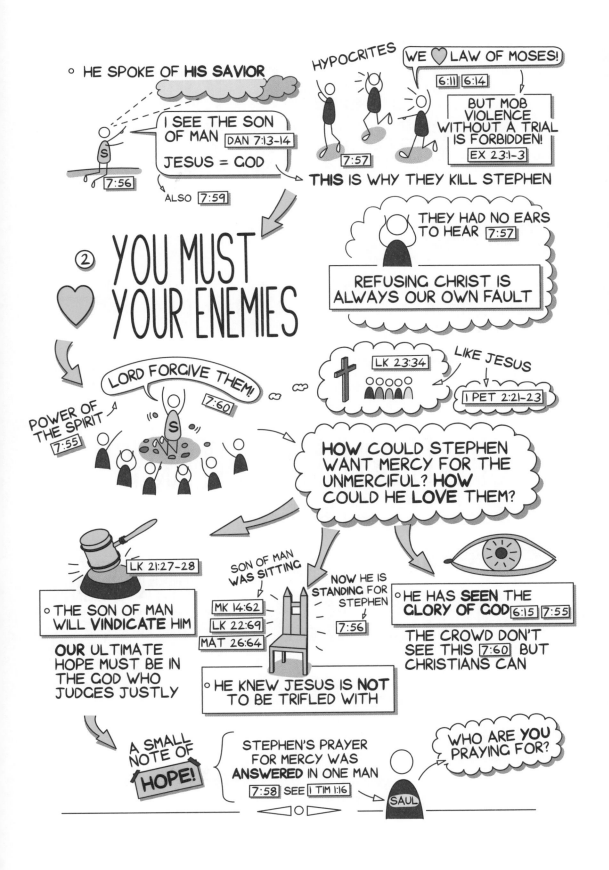

PERSECUTION LEADS TO JOY

ACTS 8:1-8

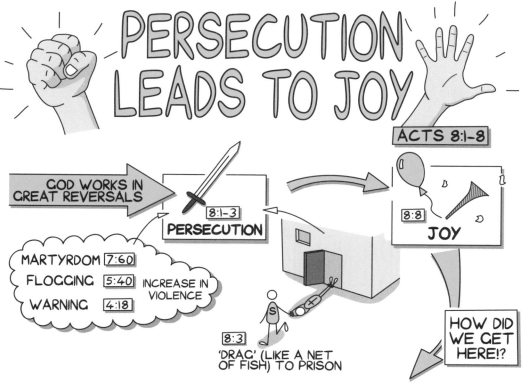

GOD WORKS IN GREAT REVERSALS

8:1-3 PERSECUTION

8:8 JOY

MARTYRDOM 7:60
FLOGGING 5:40 — INCREASE IN VIOLENCE
WARNING 4:18

8:3 'DRAG' (LIKE A NET OF FISH) TO PRISON

HOW DID WE GET HERE!?

GOD'S PEOPLE KEPT SPEAKING

8:4 NORMAL CHRISTIANS SCATTERED AND KEPT PREACHING!

ACTS 1:8 — J

JERUSALEM

ENDS OF EARTH

JUDEA

SAMARIA 8:5-8

MISSION WENT WHERE ORDINARY CHRISTIANS WENT

WHEN THE PASTOR SPEAKS OF CHRIST PEOPLE ARE NOT SURPRISED

CHRISTIANS ARE LIKE **MANURE!**

IF STAGNANT, CAN START TO STINK!

IF SPREAD OUT, VERY FRUITFUL!

MARTIN LUTHER

WHEN ANYONE ELSE DOES IT, PEOPLE ARE AMAZED!

WHAT MONEY CANNOT BUY

ACTS 8:9-25

BEWARE THINKING OF YOURSELF AS A 'SOMEBODY'

I AM GREAT!

WELL DOCUMENTED AS THE FIRST **HERETIC**

JUSTIN MARTYR
IRENAEUS
CHURCH FATHERS
HIPPOLYTUS

BAD GUY ALERT

SIMON THE 'MAGICIAN'

HE'S GREAT!

I AM GREAT! 8:9

8:10

DEALT IN BLACK MAGIC AND OCCULT

SEE DT 18:9-13

GREAT WITH A CAPITAL 'G' = "I AM DIVINE!"

8:12-13

ME NEXT!

PHILIP PREACHED AND BAPTIZED – EVEN SIMON BELIEVED AND WAS BAPTIZED!

POWER!

MIRACLES!

8:13

SIMON'S 'FAITH'

 PERCEIVED GOSPEL TO BE TRUE

CONFESSED IT TO BE TRUE

 BUT HE COULD NOT DENY HIMSELF

→ SIMON ♡ SIMON

THE GOOD NEWS ABOUT JESUS

ACTS 8:26-40

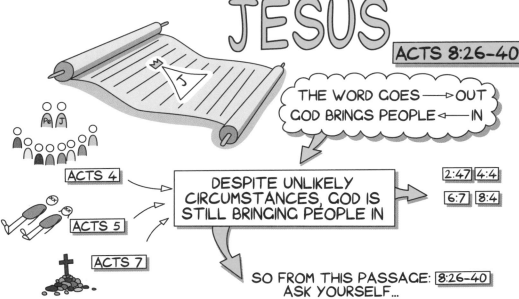

THE WORD GOES ——→ OUT
GOD BRINGS PEOPLE ←—— IN

ACTS 4

ACTS 5

ACTS 7

DESPITE UNLIKELY CIRCUMSTANCES, GOD IS STILL BRINGING PEOPLE IN

2:47 4:4
6:7 8:4

SO FROM THIS PASSAGE: 8:26-40
ASK YOURSELF...

HAVE YOU CONSIDERED WHAT GOD MAY BE ORCHESTRATING ON YOUR BEHALF?

GO SOUTH TO GAZA
8:26

PHILIP SIMPLY OBEYS
8:27

ANGEL

A DESERT PLACE

MAN STRUGGLING WITH BIBLE READING
8:28,31

DO YOU UNDERSTAND WHAT YOU ARE READING?!

EVANGELIST

NOTE: THIS WOULD HAVE TAKEN DAYS!

WHAT ARE THE CHANCES OF THIS?

6:5-6

GOD TOLD PHILIP TO LEAVE VIBRANT MINISTRY FOR ONE MAN — IS HE CALLING YOU?

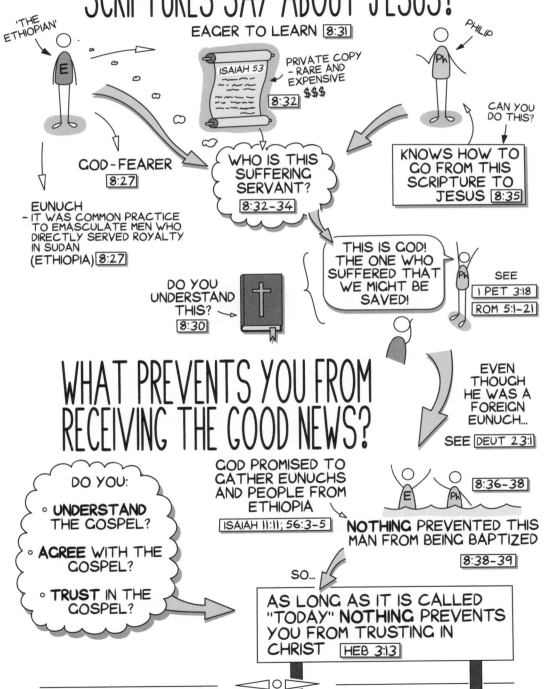

SAUL SEES THE LIGHT

ACTS 9:1-20

REPEATED IN 22:1-21 AND 26:9-18

WHAT LESSONS CAN WE LEARN ABOUT CONVERSION?

WHEN GOD SAVES SINNERS... ...NO ONE IS TOO FAR GONE

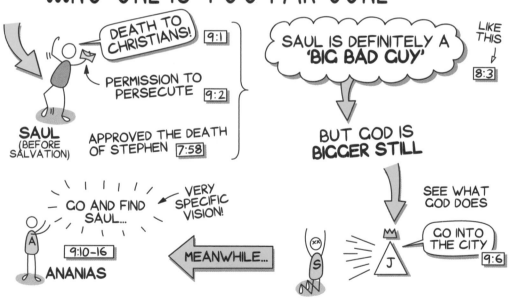

DEATH TO CHRISTIANS! 9:1

PERMISSION TO PERSECUTE 9:2

SAUL (BEFORE SALVATION)

APPROVED THE DEATH OF STEPHEN 7:58

SAUL IS DEFINITELY A 'BIG BAD GUY'

LIKE THIS 8:3

BUT GOD IS BIGGER STILL

SEE WHAT GOD DOES

GO INTO THE CITY 9:6

GO AND FIND SAUL...

VERY SPECIFIC VISION!

9:10-16

ANANIAS

MEANWHILE...

GOD DID THIS FOR ONE MAN - EVEN THE HARDEST HEART CAN BE SAVED

...HE BRINGS THEM FACE TO FACE WITH JESUS...

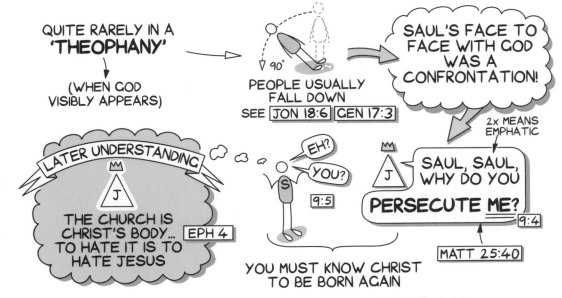

QUITE RARELY IN A **'THEOPHANY'**

(WHEN GOD VISIBLY APPEARS)

PEOPLE USUALLY FALL DOWN
SEE JON 18:6 GEN 17:3

90°

SAUL'S FACE TO FACE WITH GOD WAS A CONFRONTATION!

2x MEANS EMPHATIC

SAUL, SAUL, WHY DO YOU **PERSECUTE ME?** 9:4

MATT 25:40

LATER UNDERSTANDING

THE CHURCH IS CHRIST'S BODY... TO HATE IT IS TO HATE JESUS EPH 4

EH?

YOU? 9:5

YOU MUST KNOW CHRIST TO BE BORN AGAIN

...HE MAKES THEM A NEW PERSON AND GIVES A NEW PURPOSE...

SEE "SAUL'S" LATER WORK

2 COR 5:17
ROM 6:6
GAL 2:20

NEW PURPOSE

WE ARE ALL CALLED TO BE INSTRUMENTS FOR HIS GLORY
9:15-16 ROM 9

SAUL IS DEAD, PAUL IS ALIVE!

...HIS SAINTS BETTER BE READY

NEW PERSON

SAUL ON 'STRAIGHT' STREET (HE HAS GONE STRAIGHT!) 9:11

BROTHER SAUL 9:17 — WOW.

PROBABLY TERRIFIED

A S x x 9:18-19

IF A REPENTANT MASS-PERSECUTOR OF CHRISTIANS CAME TO YOUR CHURCH – WOULD YOU BE READY TO ACCEPT THEM?

THE HATER BECOMES THE HATED

ACTS 9:20-43

THREE REMARKABLE TRANSFORMATIONS

① SAUL 9:20-31

9:1-19

...WAS CAUSING HAVOC IN THE CHURCH

9:21   9:1-2   8:1

SAUL WAS A NATURALLY INTENSE GUY... BUT **GOD SANCTIFIES OUR ODDITIES** FOR HIS GLORY

MATT 7:15-20

NOW CAUSING HAVOC IN THE SYNAGOGUES

9:22   9:28-29

SO THE JEWS PLOTTED TO **KILL** HIM

9:23-25   9:29

EVEN YOUR CLOSEST FRIENDS AND ALLIES CAN TURN ON YOU WHEN YOU TURN TO CHRIST

MATT 10:21-22

J

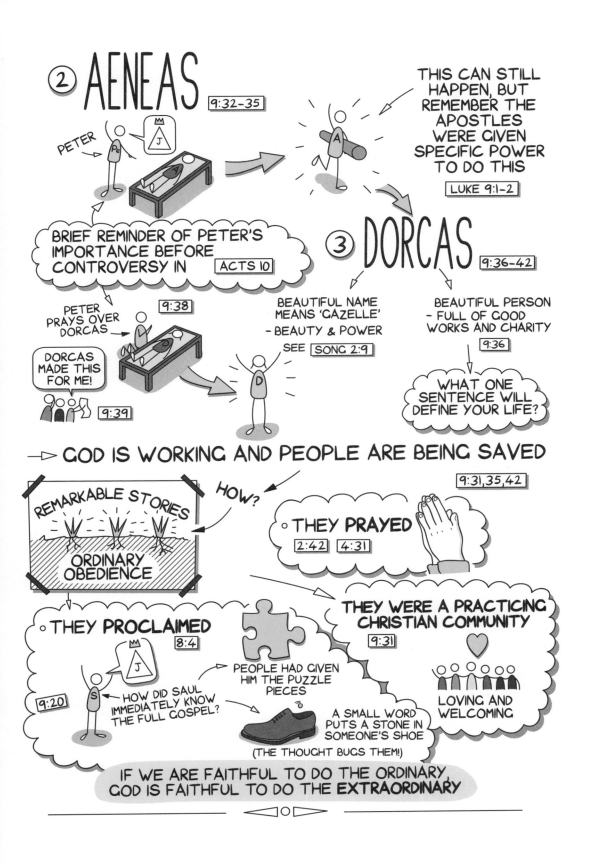

THE GOSPEL GOES TO THE GENTILES

ACTS 10:1-48

A **KEY MOMENT** FOR THE CHURCH (RETOLD THREE TIMES) `CH 10-11`

HOW CAN JEWS AND GENTILES BELONG TO THE SAME CHURCH? `CH 11`

FOR NOW → `CH 10` A FOCUS ON CORNELIUS

WHAT HE WAS

`10:1`

NAMED AFTER FAMOUS ROMAN GENERAL CORNELIUS SULLA (138-78BC)

A **CENTURION** IN CHARGE OF ONE OF 6 REGIMENTS OF 100 MEN

`10:2`

☑ **4 POSITIVES**

☑ DEVOUT MAN = VIRTUOUS, WAS GOOD IN A WORLDY SENSE

☑ FEARED GOD = GENTILE SYMPATHETIC TO JUDAISM BUT NOT A CONVERT

☑ GAVE ALMS = GENEROUS

☑ PRAYED CONTINUALLY TO GOD

OUTWARDLY DECENT GUY

AT HEART, IN REBELLION AGAINST GOD

APPRECIATE HIS GOODNESS, BUT DON'T DILUTE YOUR THEOLOGY!

`10:22` SUMMARY STATEMENT

ORIGINAL SIN

TOTAL DEPRAVITY

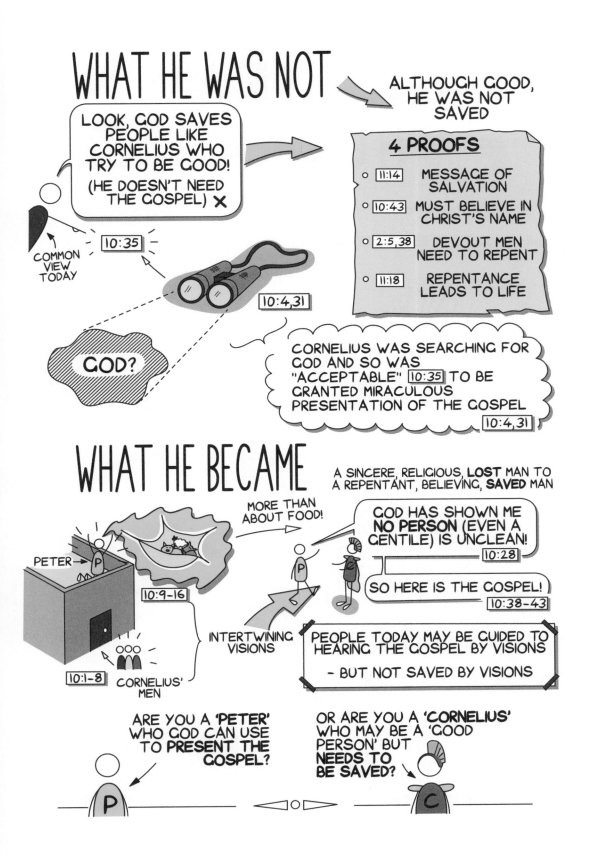

REPENTANCE UNTO LIFE

ACTS 11:1-18

WHAT DOES THE STORY OF CORNELIUS MEAN FOR THE CHURCH?

10:1-48

THE CHALLENGE

THE NEWS OF CORNELIUS GOT TO JERUSALEM BEFORE PETER!

11:1

GRR!

PETER MET BY 'CIRCUMCISION PARTY' } VERY PARTICULAR ABOUT JEWISH CUSTOMS

YOU'RE EATING GENTILE FOOD AND HAVING GENTILE FELLOWSHIP!

11:3

THIS IS NOT SIMPLY PRIDE...

THIS VIEWPOINT CAME FROM GOD!

YOU ARE MY HOLY NATION

EX 19:3-6
EX 20:3

MEANS 'SET APART'

SINAI

YOU MUST NOT EAT LIKE THE NATIONS!

LEV 22-26

DO NOT BE JOINED TO THEM DT 7:1-5

LATER... EVEN PETER STRUGGLES WITH THIS

GAL 2:11-16

Pe

FELLOWSHIP WITH GENTILES WAS A HUGE CHALLENGE

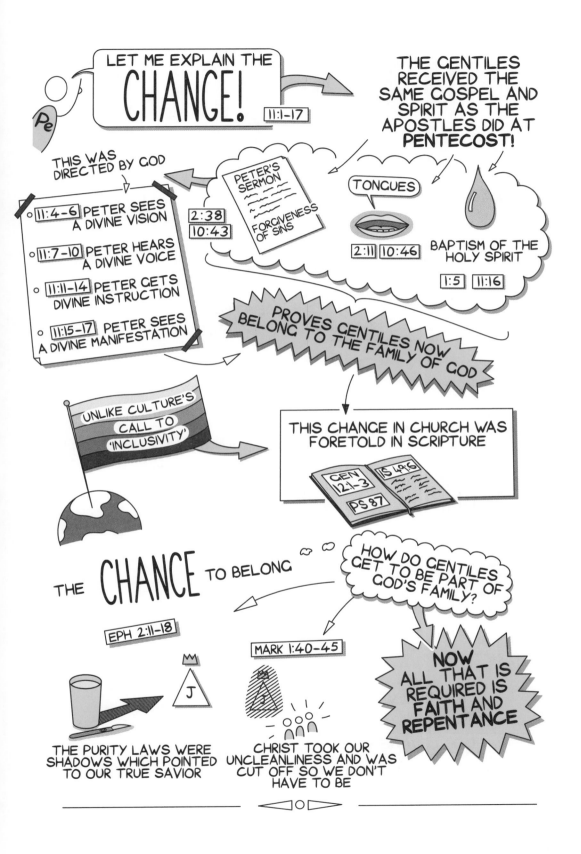

THE HAND OF THE LORD WAS WITH THEM

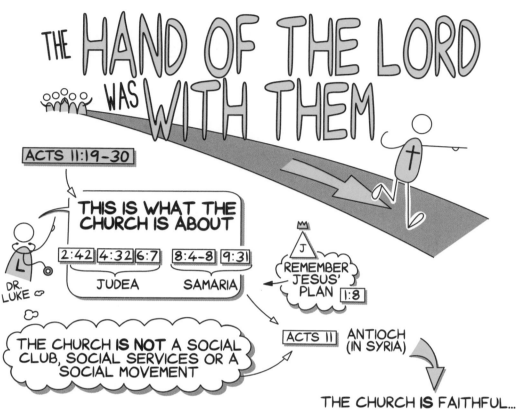

ACTS 11:19-30

THIS IS WHAT THE CHURCH IS ABOUT

2:42 4:32 6:7   8:4-8 9:31

JUDEA   SAMARIA

DR. LUKE

REMEMBER JESUS' PLAN 1:8

THE CHURCH IS NOT A SOCIAL CLUB, SOCIAL SERVICES OR A SOCIAL MOVEMENT

ACTS 11   ANTIOCH (IN SYRIA)

THE CHURCH IS FAITHFUL...

FAITHFUL TO EVANGELIZE

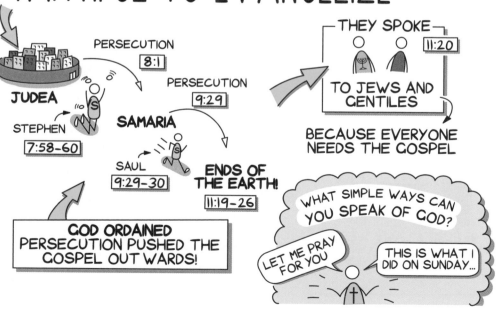

PERSECUTION 8:1

JUDEA

STEPHEN 7:58-60

PERSECUTION 9:29

SAMARIA

SAUL 9:29-30

ENDS OF THE EARTH! 11:19-26

THEY SPOKE 11:20

TO JEWS AND GENTILES

BECAUSE EVERYONE NEEDS THE GOSPEL

GOD ORDAINED PERSECUTION PUSHED THE GOSPEL OUTWARDS!

WHAT SIMPLE WAYS CAN YOU SPEAK OF GOD?

LET ME PRAY FOR YOU

THIS IS WHAT I DID ON SUNDAY...

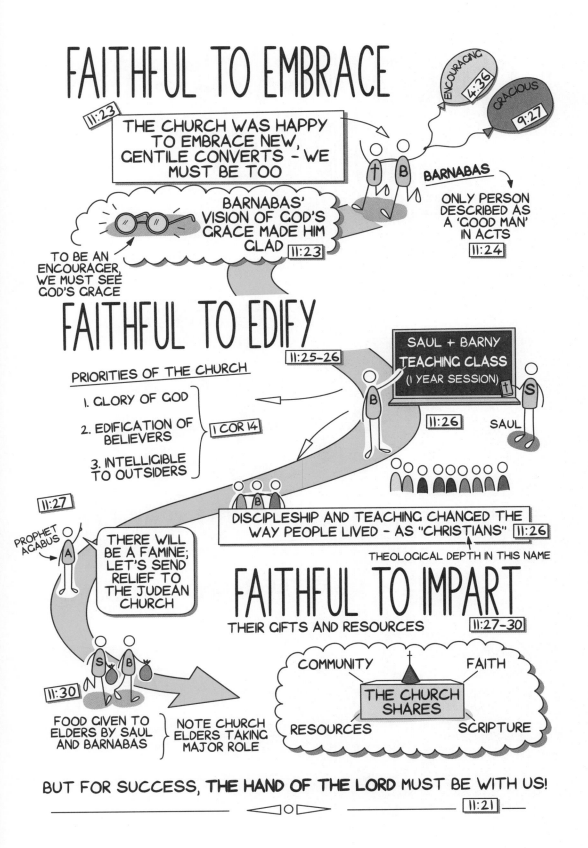

THE CHURCH IN EARNEST PRAYER

ACTS 12:1-19

WHY CHAPTER 12?

GOD IS SOVEREIGN OVER NATIONS AND **INDIVIDUALS**

SAUL AND BARNABAS 12:25

SAUL AND BARNABAS 11:30

12:1-24 PETER RESCUED

?

THE WORD KEEPS GOING OUT 12:24

REMEMBER: WE GET A 'GOD'S EYE VIEW' – THE INDIVIDUALS MAY HAVE ONLY SEEN FAILURE 12:1-2 9:23 8:1 7:58 ...

THERE IS A BATTLE RAGING!

REV 13   EPH 6:12
1 PET 5:8

Vs

THE WORLD
- KING HEROD
- VIOLENCE TO THE CHURCH 12:1
- HATRED FROM JEWISH LEADERS
- JAMES KILLED 12:2
- PETER CHAINED, BEHIND BARS AND GUARDED BY 4 SQUADS OF SOLDIERS...

THE CHURCH
- EARNEST PRAYER 12:5

BUT GOD LAUGHS! PS 2

WHAT DID THIS PRAYER LOOK LIKE?

BE CAREFUL WITH YOUR GLORY!

ACTS 12:20-25

ARE YOU A GLORY THIEF?

THE WORST KIND OF THIEF

THERE ARE SEVERE CONSEQUENCES TO STEALING GOD'S GLORY

IS 48:11

(IT IS OF ULTIMATE VALUE)

HEROD AGRIPPA 12:1

(GRANDSON OF HEROD THE GREAT) MATT 2

- MURDERER 12:2
- PANDERER 12:3
- CRUEL 12:19
- ANGRY 12:20

12:20

x SIDON

x TYRE

RULED BY AGRIPPA

MAP OF PALESTINE AROUND AD 40

HISTORICAL ACCOUNT

JOSEPHUS ANTIQUITES 19

KING'S CHAMBERLAIN, BLASTUS

BL

TYRE AND SIDON ASK FOR PEACE (THEY NEED HEROD FOR SURVIVAL)

SPARKLING CLOTHING

GRANDIOSE SPEECH 12:21

PUNISHMENT:

DID NOT CORRECT THEM!

YOU ARE A GOD! 12:22

DEATH 12:23

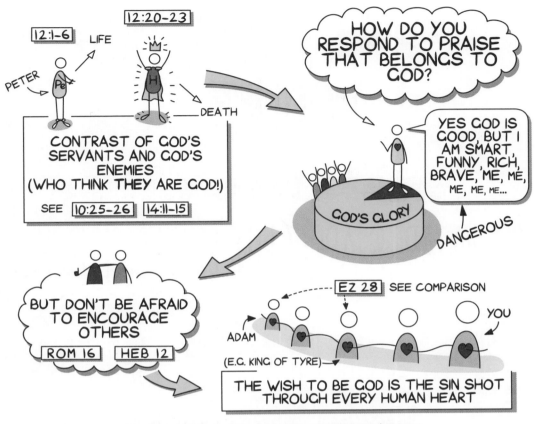

GOD MUST CHANGE OUR HEARTS TO MAKE US LIKE **CHRIST**, NOT LIKE **HEROD**

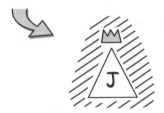

- IS DEITY BUT DID NOT USE HIS POWER SELF-SERVINGLY [PHIL 2:5-11]
- SUFFERED FOR HIS ENEMIES [1 PET 3:18]
- WAS A POOR MAN [LUK 9:58]
- ASCENDED TO GLORY [2:23]

- THOUGHT HIMSELF DEITY AND TRIED TO USE THIS POWER [12:22]
- CAUSED ENEMIES TO SUFFER [12:1]
- DRESSED LIKE A KING [12:21]
- EATEN BY WORMS [12:23]

WHOSE GLORY WILL YOU LIVE FOR?

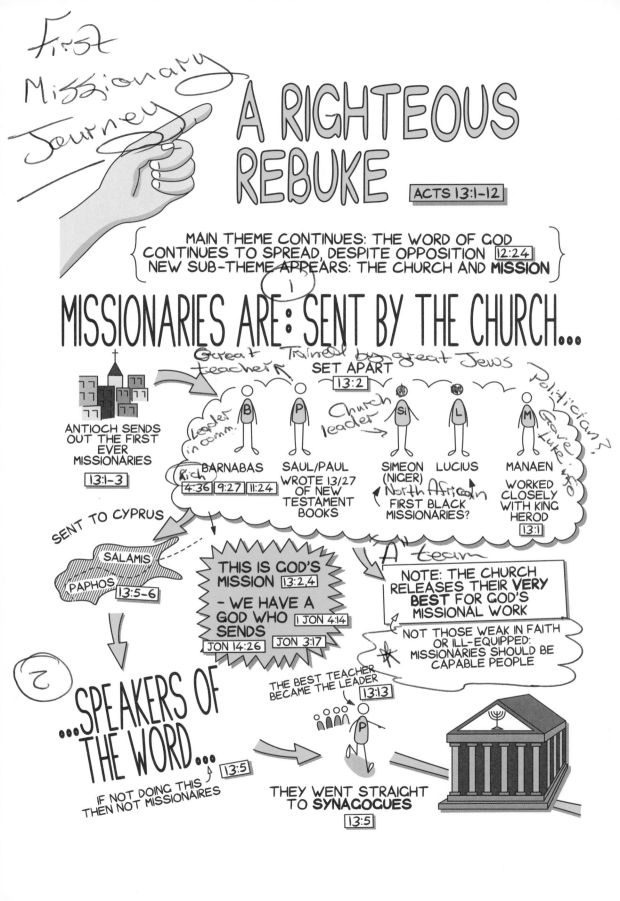

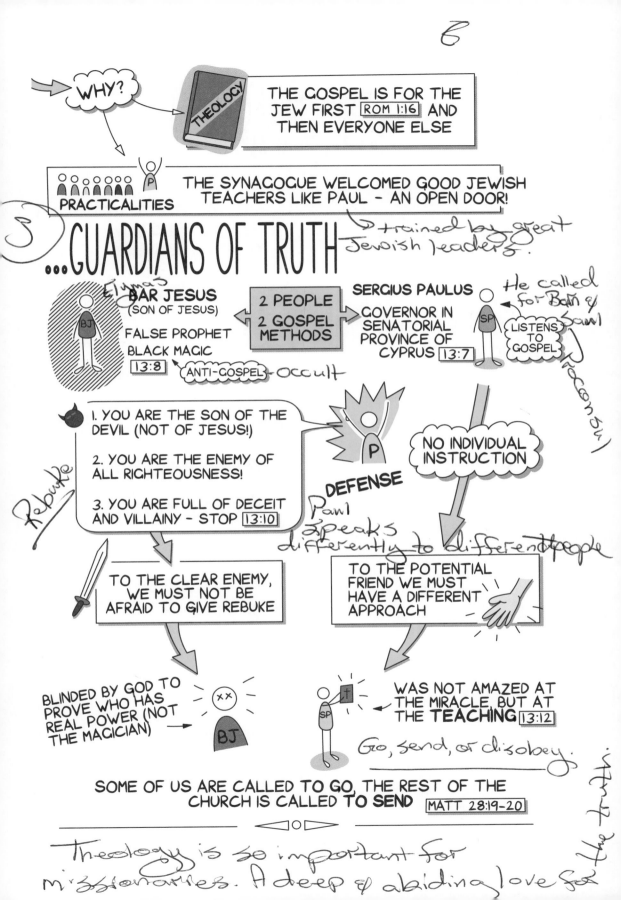

WHY?

THEOLOGY

THE GOSPEL IS FOR THE JEW FIRST ROM 1:16 AND THEN EVERYONE ELSE

PRACTICALITIES

THE SYNAGOGUE WELCOMED GOOD JEWISH TEACHERS LIKE PAUL — AN OPEN DOOR!

→ trained by great Jewish leaders.

...GUARDIANS OF TRUTH

Elymas
BAR JESUS (SON OF JESUS)

FALSE PROPHET BLACK MAGIC 13:8

ANTI-GOSPEL — occult

2 PEOPLE
2 GOSPEL METHODS

SERGIUS PAULUS
GOVERNOR IN SENATORIAL PROVINCE OF CYPRUS 13:7

He called for Barn & Saul

LISTENS TO GOSPEL

Proconsul

1. YOU ARE THE SON OF THE DEVIL (NOT OF JESUS!)

2. YOU ARE THE ENEMY OF ALL RIGHTEOUSNESS!

3. YOU ARE FULL OF DECEIT AND VILLAINY — STOP 13:10

Rebuke

DEFENSE

NO INDIVIDUAL INSTRUCTION

Paul speaks differently to different people

TO THE CLEAR ENEMY, WE MUST NOT BE AFRAID TO GIVE REBUKE

TO THE POTENTIAL FRIEND WE MUST HAVE A DIFFERENT APPROACH

BLINDED BY GOD TO PROVE WHO HAS REAL POWER (NOT THE MAGICIAN) → BJ

WAS NOT AMAZED AT THE MIRACLE, BUT AT THE TEACHING 13:12

SP

Go, send, or disobey.

SOME OF US ARE CALLED TO GO, THE REST OF THE CHURCH IS CALLED TO SEND MATT 28:19-20

Theology is so important for missionaries. A deep & abiding love for the truth.

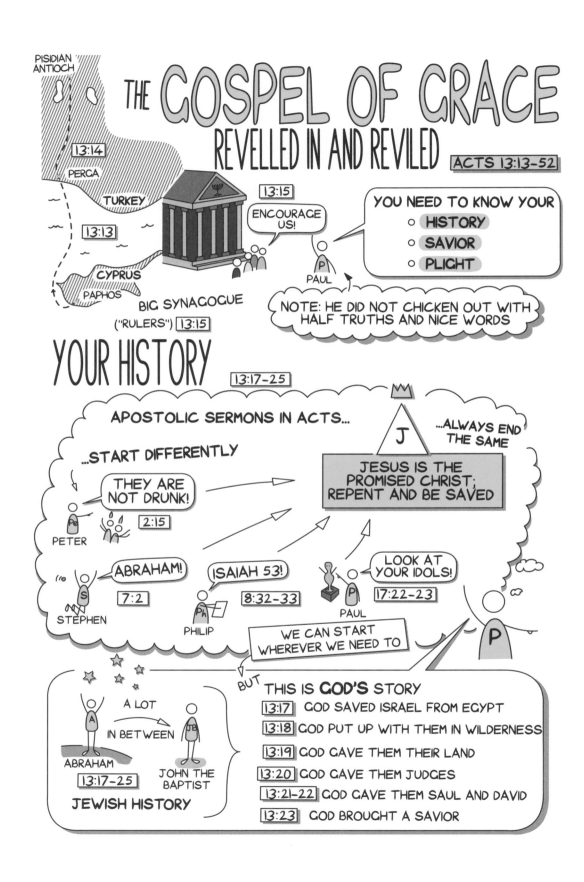

A PEOPLE DIVIDED

ACTS 14:1-7

PISIDIAN ANTIOCH

ICONIUM

TURKEY

JEWS & GENTILES

WE ARE SHOWN 3 TYPICAL ASPECTS OF MINISTRY THAT WE SHOULD EXPECT ON MISSION

THE APOSTLES' TYPICAL STRATEGY

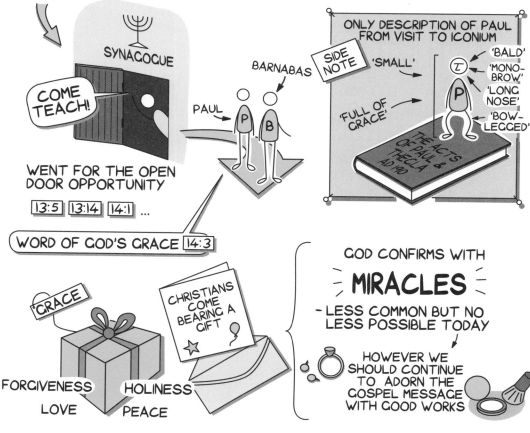

SYNAGOGUE

COME TEACH!

BARNABAS

PAUL

SIDE NOTE

WENT FOR THE OPEN DOOR OPPORTUNITY

13:5 13:14 14:1 ...

WORD OF GOD'S GRACE 14:3

ONLY DESCRIPTION OF PAUL FROM VISIT TO ICONIUM

'SMALL'

'FULL OF GRACE'

'BALD'

'MONO-BROW'

'LONG NOSE'

'BOW-LEGGED'

THE ACTS OF PAUL & THECLA AD 190

'GRACE

CHRISTIANS COME BEARING A GIFT

FORGIVENESS

LOVE

HOLINESS

PEACE

GOD CONFIRMS WITH

MIRACLES

- LESS COMMON BUT NO LESS POSSIBLE TODAY

HOWEVER WE SHOULD CONTINUE TO ADORN THE GOSPEL MESSAGE WITH GOOD WORKS

THE CITY'S TYPICAL RESPONSE

SOME BELIEVED

OTHERS HATED

TYPICAL:

4:1-4	5:12-16
6:7-11	9:28-31
13:42-45	14:4

COMMON OPINION TODAY

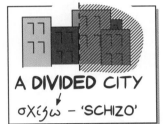

A DIVIDED CITY

σχίςω - 'SCHIZO'

BUT IF EVERYONE JUST HEARD OF JESUS' LOVE THERE WOULD BE PEACE!

WRONG

J

MY GOSPEL WILL **DIVIDE** THE WORLD

LUK 2:34-35

LUK 12:49

MATT 25:42

A BAD REACTION TO THE GOSPEL DOES NOT MEAN IT HAS BEEN MISUNDERSTOOD

14:2,19

IN FACT, IT CAN BE A SIGN THAT THE TRUE GOSPEL HAS BEEN HEARD

THE CHURCH'S TYPICAL RESOLVE

THEY FACED OPPOSITION "SO" STAYED FOR SOME TIME...

14:2-3

STRANGE

...BUT **LEFT** WHEN THEIR LIVES WERE THREATENED

14:5-6

WHETHER BY **LIFE** ROM 14:8 OR BY **DEATH** ACTS 7 WE MUST DO ALL THINGS **FOR THE GOOD OF THE GOSPEL**

WE HAVE OTHER PLACES TO PREACH!

SAME NATURE BETTER NEWS

ACTS 14:8-18

JESUS SAVES

THE WORLD

- YOU CAN'T BE KNOWLEDGEABLE **AND** HUMBLE
- BEING HUMBLE IS SAYING 'I'M NOT CERTAIN'

VS

- YOU SHOULD BE HUMBLE AND CONFIDENT IN KNOWING GOD

| PROV 29:23 | HEB 4:16 |
| EPH 4:2 | PHIL 4:13 |

THE BIBLE

CHRISTIANS ARE NORMAL PEOPLE WITH BETTER NEWS

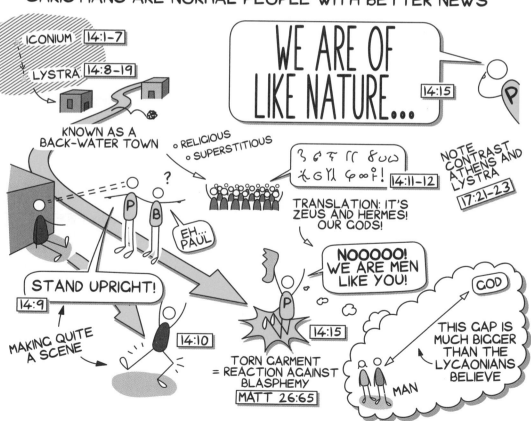

ICONIUM 14:1-7

LYSTRA 14:8-19

KNOWN AS A BACK-WATER TOWN

WE ARE OF LIKE NATURE...
14:15

P

- RELIGIOUS
- SUPERSTITIOUS

3 ଫ ୫ ୮୮ ୪୰ 大 ୠ୲ ୶∞ᵒᵢ! 14:11-12

TRANSLATION: IT'S ZEUS AND HERMES! OUR GODS!

NOTE CONTRAST ATHENS AND LYSTRA 17:21-23

NOOOOO! WE ARE MEN LIKE YOU!

? EH... PAUL

P B

STAND UPRIGHT! 14:9

MAKING QUITE A SCENE

14:10

P

14:15

TORN GARMENT = REACTION AGAINST BLASPHEMY MATT 26:65

GOD

THIS GAP IS MUCH BIGGER THAN THE LYCAONIANS BELIEVE

MAN

THE THREE-LEGGED STOOL OF MISSION

WHAT DO MISSIONARIES DO? ACTS 14:19-28

MISSIONARIES ARE **SENT ONES:**

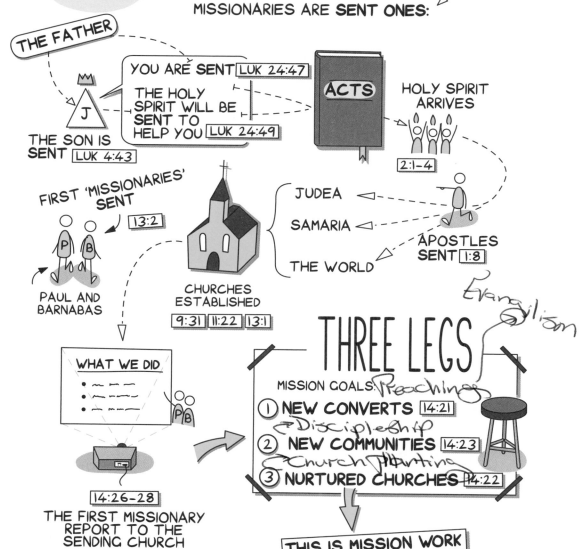

THE FATHER

YOU ARE SENT LUK 24:47

THE HOLY SPIRIT WILL BE SENT TO HELP YOU LUK 24:49

THE SON IS SENT LUK 4:43

ACTS

HOLY SPIRIT ARRIVES

2:1-4

FIRST 'MISSIONARIES' SENT

13:2

PAUL AND BARNABAS

JUDEA

SAMARIA

THE WORLD

APOSTLES SENT 1:8

CHURCHES ESTABLISHED

9:31 11:22 13:1

WHAT WE DID
- ‒‒‒‒
- ‒‒‒‒
- ‒‒‒‒

14:26-28

THE FIRST MISSIONARY REPORT TO THE SENDING CHURCH

THREE LEGS

Evangilism

MISSION GOALS: Preaching

① NEW CONVERTS 14:21
   ↪ Discipleship

② NEW COMMUNITIES 14:23
   ↪ Church Planting

③ NURTURED CHURCHES 14:22

THIS IS MISSION WORK

CONVERTS   COMMUNITIES   CHURCHES

NOT JUST ABOUT MAKING NEW CONVERTS

ROM 1:1

PAUL

MISSIONARIES MAY FOCUS MORE ON ONE ASPECT OVER ANOTHER – BUT ALL ARE NEEDED!

NOT JUST ABOUT COMMUNITY DEVELOPMENT

THE WORK OF MISSION IS PRIMARILY TO **ADVANCE THE GOSPEL!**

WHAT DO MISSIONARIES DO?

1. PREACH THE GOSPEL TO THOSE WHO HAVEN'T HEARD
2. DISCIPLE NEW BELIEVERS IN LIFE AND DOCTRINE
3. ESTABLISH THESE DISCIPLES IN HEALTHY CHURCHES

THREE IMPLICATIONS

HOW DO YOU COMPARE?

 ACTS 14

ACTS 14 IS A DIAGNOSTIC TOOL FOR MISSIONARIES

WHERE IS GREATEST NEED?

WHAT ARE YOUR STRENGTHS?

CHURCHES SHOULD SUPPORT MISSIONS WHICH FOLLOW THESE GUIDELINES

 I MUST GO!

ARE YOU BEING CALLED TO MISSION?

14:22 REMEMBER: THE CALL IS TO **SUFFER**; MISSIONARIES MUST BE PREPARED ESPECIALLY WELL

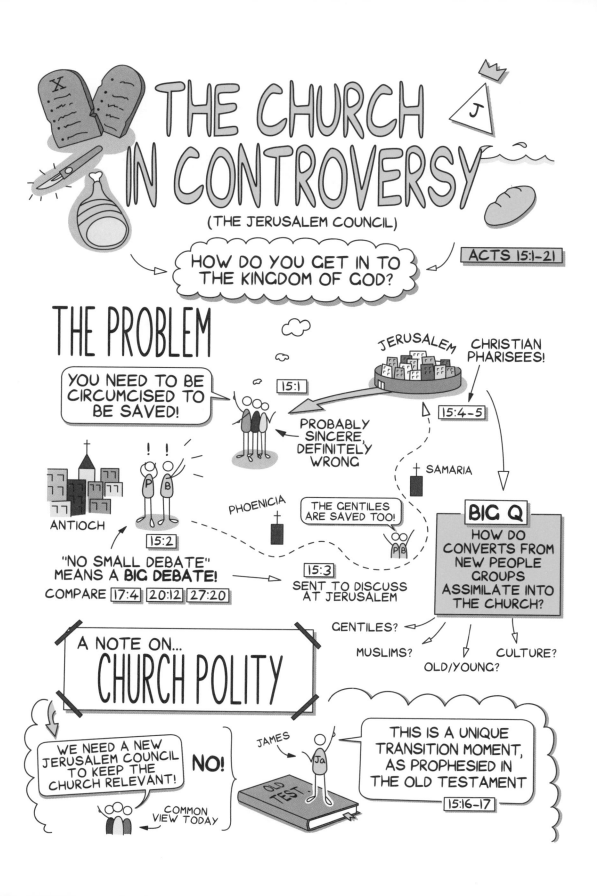

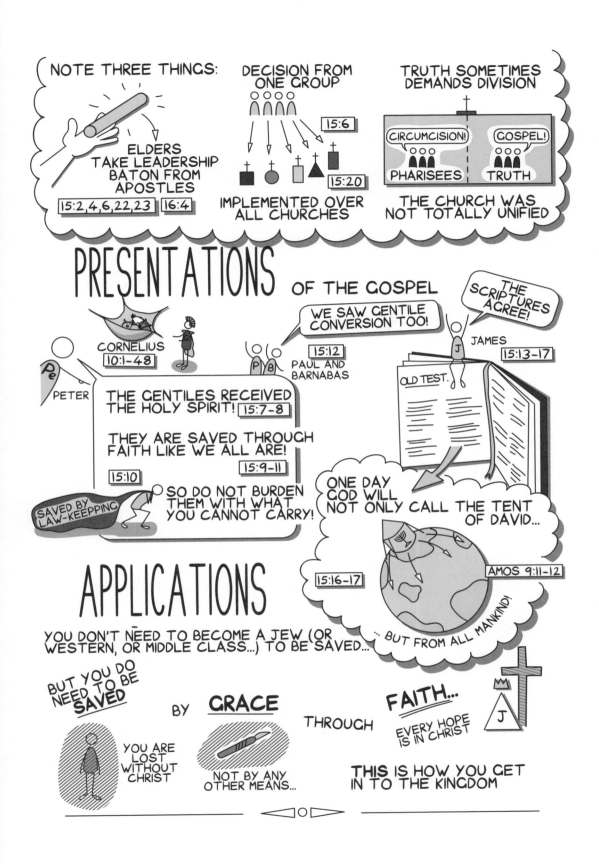

CONTROVERSY SETTLED?

WHAT CHRISTIANS MUST LEAVE BEHIND

ACTS 15:19-35

JAMES

LET US WRITE A LETTER!

15:19-20

DELIVERED TO **ALL** CHURCHES

16:4

BY

Dear Churches...
DO NOT WORRY
YOU DO NOT NEED TO BE CIRCUMCISED TO BE SAVED 15:1-20
- YOU ONLY NEED GRACE BY FAITH

HOWEVER, YOU SHOULD ABSTAIN FROM THE FOLLOWING:

15:19-20, 28-29
21:25

THE POLLUTION OF IDOLS

FROM BLOOD

MEAT FROM STRANGLED ANIMALS

SEXUAL IMMORALITY

PB
PAUL & BARNABAS

S Ba
SILAS & BARSABBAS

15:22

FROM JERUSALEM CHURCHES

FROM ANTIOCH CHURCHES

WHY THESE FOUR THINGS?

THEY DESCRIBE

PAGAN WORSHIP

A SIGN OF TOTAL CHURCH UNITY ON THIS DECISION

SEE DESCRIPTION:

2ND MACCABEES CH 6

DRINKING PARTIES SEXUAL IMMORALITY, DISTURBING RITUALS...

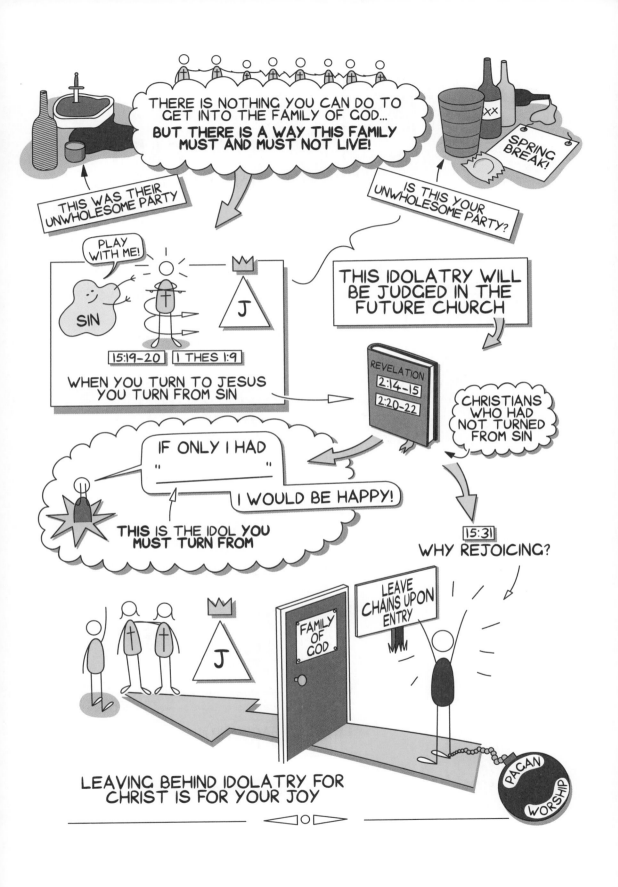

CHRISTIANS IN CONFLICT

ACTS 15:36-41

> THERE ARE ALWAYS CONFLICTS IN THE CHURCH BECAUSE CHRISTIANS **ARE STILL SINNERS**

CONFLICT IS...

FREQUENTLY SURPRISING

TWO DEVOUT CHRISTIANS,

PAUL   BARNABAS

WROTE 13 NEW TESTAMENT BOOKS

INCREDIBLE CONVERSION 9:1-19

GAVE HIS LIFE FOR MISSION

2 COR 11:24-28

SON OF ENCOURAGEMENT 4:36

FULL OF THE HOLY SPIRIT AND OF FAITH 11:23-24

BUT CONFLICT IS OFTEN OVER THE

'SMALL' STUFF

WHO HAVE BEEN THROUGH **SO MUCH!**

PAUL   BARNY

- BARNABAS TRUSTED IN PAUL 9:27
- FIRST MISSIONARY PAIR 13:2
- WENT THROUGH MUCH PAIN TOGETHER 14:19-22
- SAME DEBATING TEAM 15:2,12

15:36

ANTIOCH

LET'S GO BACK AND BUILD UP THE CHURCHES WE ESTABLISHED

ACTS 13-14

P

OK, LET'S TAKE JOHN MARK 15:37

B

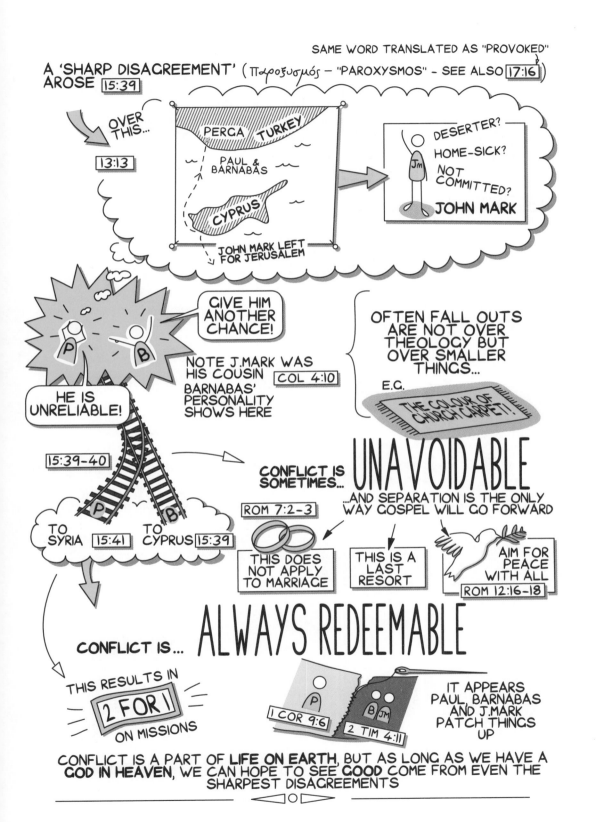

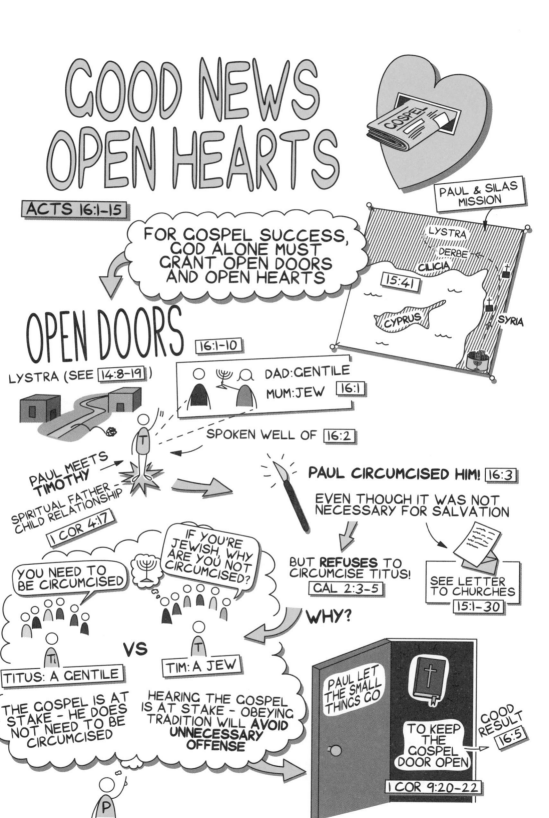

WHAT MUST I DO TO BE SAVED?

ACTS 16:16-40

THE GOSPEL ADVANCES IN PHILIPPI - **4 SCENES**

① **LYDIA**
16:11-15

② **DEMON POSSESSED GIRL**
16:16-24

SPIRIT OF 'DIVINATION' IN GREEK πύθων - PYTHON

POWER BELIEVED BY LOCALS TO COME FROM GREEK GOD **PYTHON**

FORBIDDEN

DT 18:10   1 SAM 15:23

IT IS AN ATTEMPT TO MANIPULATE GOD

POWER COMES FROM DEMONS

THESE ARE SERVANTS OF GOD!

SEE MARK 1:23-24

16:17

P S

PAUL

COME OUT OF HER!

16:18

MANY DAYS LATER

THE GOSPEL IS NOT GOOD NEWS FOR THE ENEMIES OF GOD

16:20-24

GO TO JAIL

SLAVERS

16:19

③ **THE MAGISTRATES**
16:35-40

YOU MAGISTRATES JAILED AND BEAT **INNOCENT ROMAN CITIZENS**, COME THROW US OUT YOURSELVES!

16:37

ROMANS! EEK!

16:38

ROMAN CITIZENS HAD RIGHTS - THEY WERE ABUSED HERE

NOT PAUL'S PRIDE, BUT HE WANTED THE GOSPEL TO BE **PUBLICLY VINDICATED**

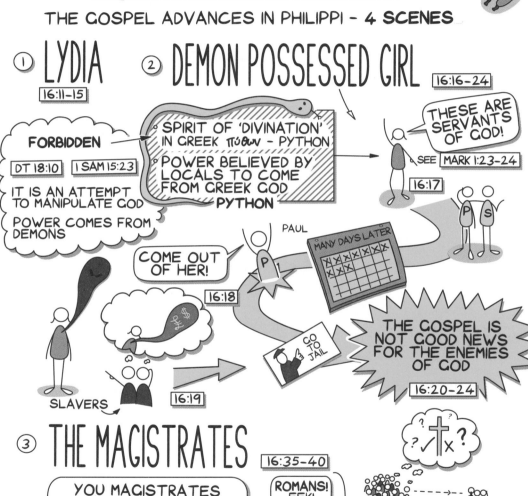

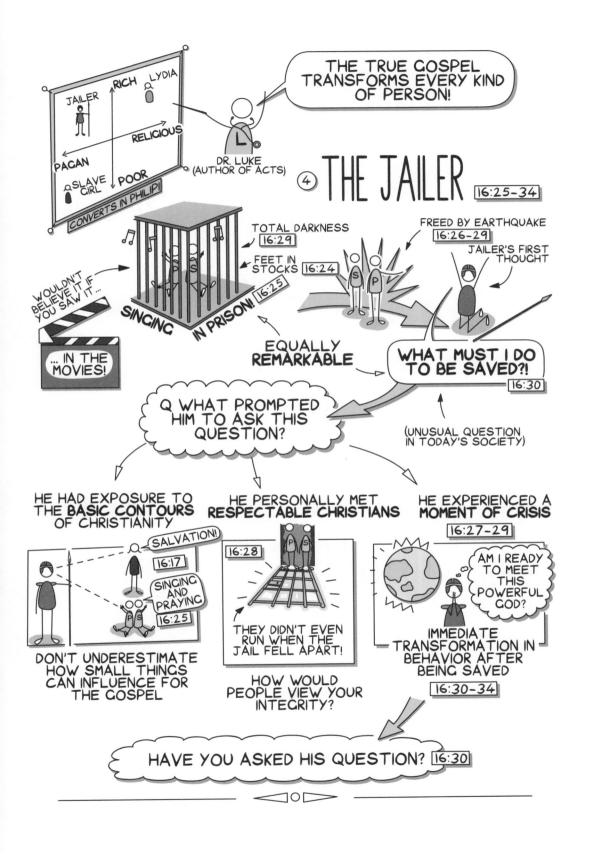

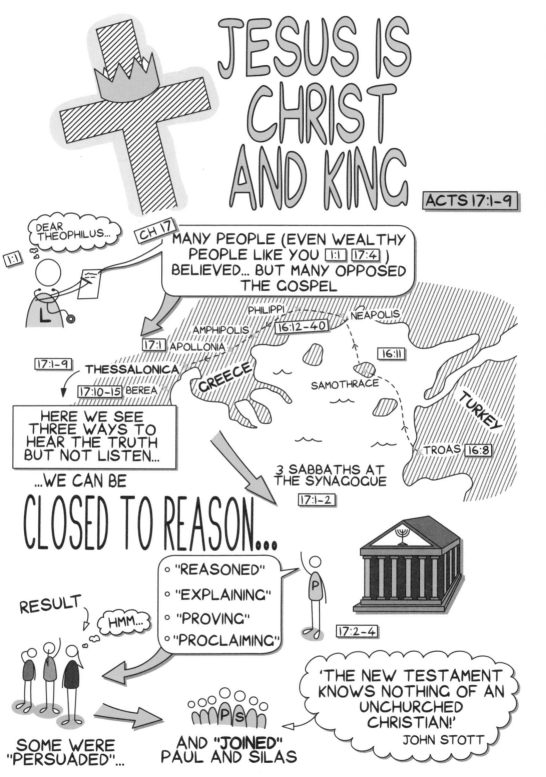

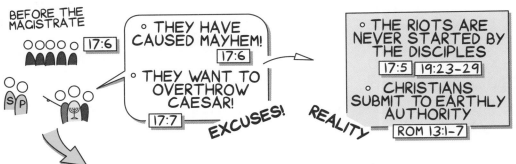

PEOPLE OF THE BOOK

ACTS 17:10-15

2 DAY JOURNEY

THESSALONICA

BEREA

WILFULLY IGNORANT AND VIOLENT
17:5

VS

17:11

HMM...

THE BEREANS WERE MORE **NOBLE**

THE JEWS FROM THESSALONICA TRAVELED TO BEREA **JUST** TO OPPOSE GOD'S MESSAGE
17:13

THEY CHECKED WHAT PAUL TAUGHT AGAINST THE **SCRIPTURES**

TEN WAYS TO BE NOBLE
LIKE THE BEREANS

① LISTEN TO THE SERMON WITH AN **OPEN BIBLE**

DON'T TRUST ME: TRUST THE **BIBLE**!

TRUE PREACHING COMES FROM SCRIPTURE
NEH 8:8

② **DON'T RUSH** FROM THE WORD OF GOD TO THE REST OF YOUR LIFE

WORRIES OF LIFE
MATT 13:7,22

UNHINDERED TIME WITH THE WORD

THE WORD OF GOD IS NOT A MICROWAVE MEAL — IT NEEDS **TIME TO COOK**

LESSONS IN ACCOMMODATION AND CONFRONTATION

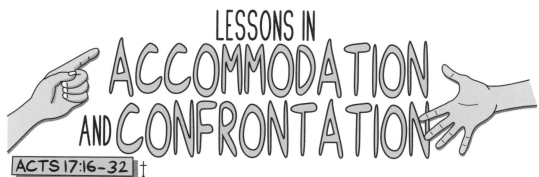

ACTS 17:16-32

AS THE GAP BETWEEN THE CHURCH AND THE WORLD GROWS, WE BECOME MORE LIKE THE CHURCH IN ACTS

SO HOW SHOULD CHRISTIANS ENGAGE WITH CULTURE?

ANTICIPATE COLLISIONS

ATHENS: THE CAMBRIDGE OF GREECE

17:10-15
BEREA

GREECE

ATHENS
17:15-34

17:16

17:17

1 PET 4:12

DON'T BE SURPRISED!

PAUL PROVOKED BY MANY IDOLS

THE FIRST CULTURAL COLLISION IS IN OUR MINDS PS 69:9; 119:136

DO WE CARE ABOUT IDOLATRY?

SO PAUL REASONED IN THE SYNAGOGUES AND MARKETPLACE

THE 'GODS' ARE DISTANT - ENJOY LIFE BECAUSE WE DIE SOON!

GOD IS FOUND IN EVERYTHING BE GOOD AND DUTIFUL

CHRISTIANITY IS A MADE UP, WEIRD PHILOSOPHY!

COMMON TODAY

EPICUREANS

17:18
THIS MAY BE HOW PEOPLE VIEW YOUR FAITH TODAY

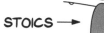
STOICS

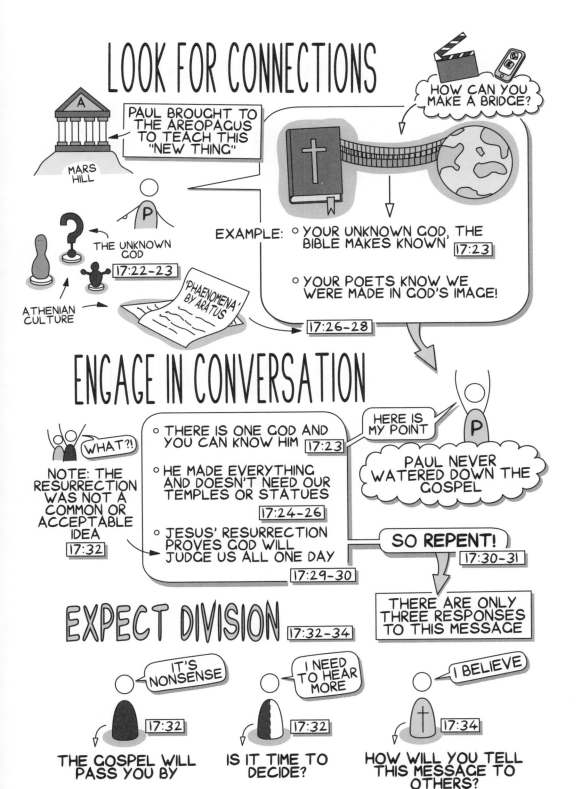

SOVEREIGN FUEL FOR MINISTRY FAITHFULNESS

ACTS 18:1-11

THE GOAL OF MINISTRY

WELL DONE GOOD AND FAITHFUL SERVANT

J

IS TO BE **FAITHFUL**

BUT WHAT DOES FAITHFULNESS REQUIRE?

IT REQUIRES:

HARD WORK AND PERSONAL SACRIFICE...

CORINTH

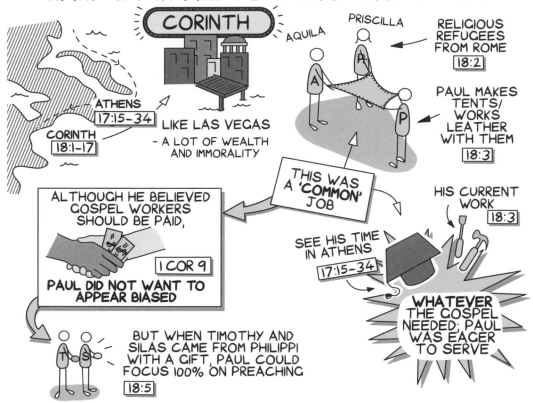

ATHENS 17:15-34

CORINTH 18:1-17

LIKE LAS VEGAS
- A LOT OF WEALTH AND IMMORALITY

AQUILA

PRISCILLA

RELIGIOUS REFUGEES FROM ROME 18:2

PAUL MAKES TENTS/ WORKS LEATHER WITH THEM 18:3

THIS WAS A 'COMMON' JOB

HIS CURRENT WORK 18:3

ALTHOUGH HE BELIEVED GOSPEL WORKERS SHOULD BE PAID,

1 COR 9

PAUL DID NOT WANT TO APPEAR BIASED

SEE HIS TIME IN ATHENS 17:15-34

WHATEVER THE GOSPEL NEEDED, PAUL WAS EAGER TO SERVE

BUT WHEN TIMOTHY AND SILAS CAME FROM PHILIPPI WITH A GIFT, PAUL COULD FOCUS 100% ON PREACHING 18:5

FOR THE SAKE OF THE GOSPEL, PAUL WORKED HARD TO
REMOVE ANY BARRIERS FOR HIS LISTENERS

...SAYING WHAT NEEDS TO BE SAID...
18:6

(EVEN WHEN NOBODY WANTS TO HEAR IT)

18:5

BOO!

P

FINE, I HAVE
WARNED YOU;
NOW I GO TO
THE GENTILES!

18:6

CHRISTIANS
ARE
WATCHMEN AT
THE GATE
-WE ARE
RESPONSIBLE

EZ 33:1-9

DO YOU EVER SPEAK ABOUT THE HARD PARTS OF SCRIPTURE?

...FULLY BELIEVING THE PROMISES OF GOD

18:8

18:7

SO PAUL WENT
TO THE HOUSE
OF TITIUS
JUSTUS
NEXT DOOR!

THE SYNAGOGUE
LEADER BELIEVED
AND CAME TOO!

P

THINGS ARE
GETTING
SCARY HERE...

18:9

GOD

KEEP GOING PAUL;
I PROMISE YOU MY
○ PRESENCE   18:10
○ PROTECTION 18:10
○ PROVIDENTIAL CARE 18:10

GOD GIVES US SIMILAR PROMISES

PRESENCE

PS 23:4

I AM ALWAYS
WITH YOU

MATT 28:20   J

PROTECTION

MATT 10:29-31

ROM 8

J

NOTHING WILL
SEPARATE US

PROVIDENTIAL CARE

IS 40:8; 55:11

GOD WILL MAKE
HIS WORD
FRUITFUL

BECAUSE GOD HAS CHOSEN SOME TO BELIEVE, WE CAN
KEEP SPEAKING IN CONFIDENCE

◁○▷

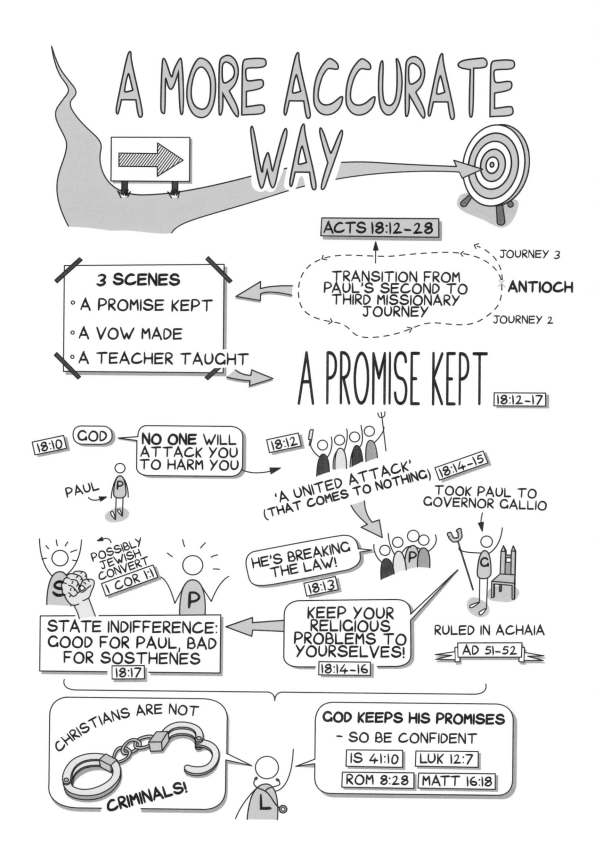

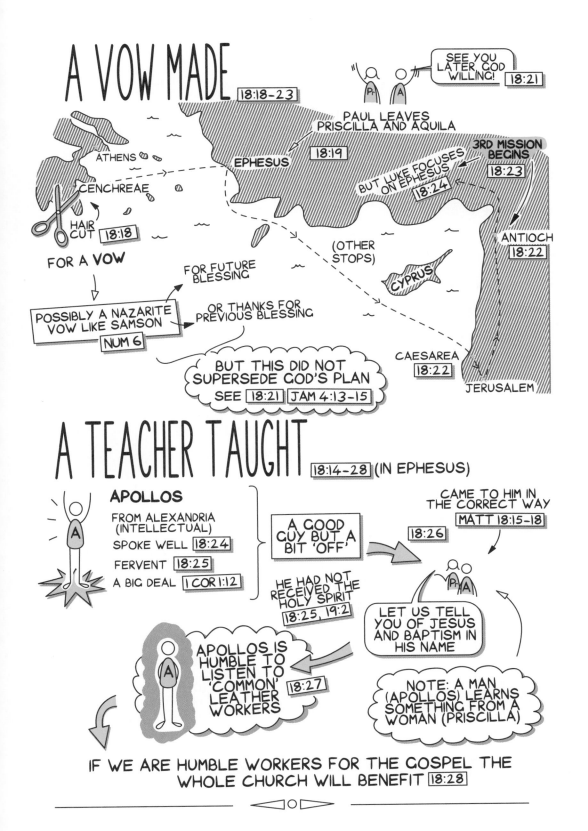

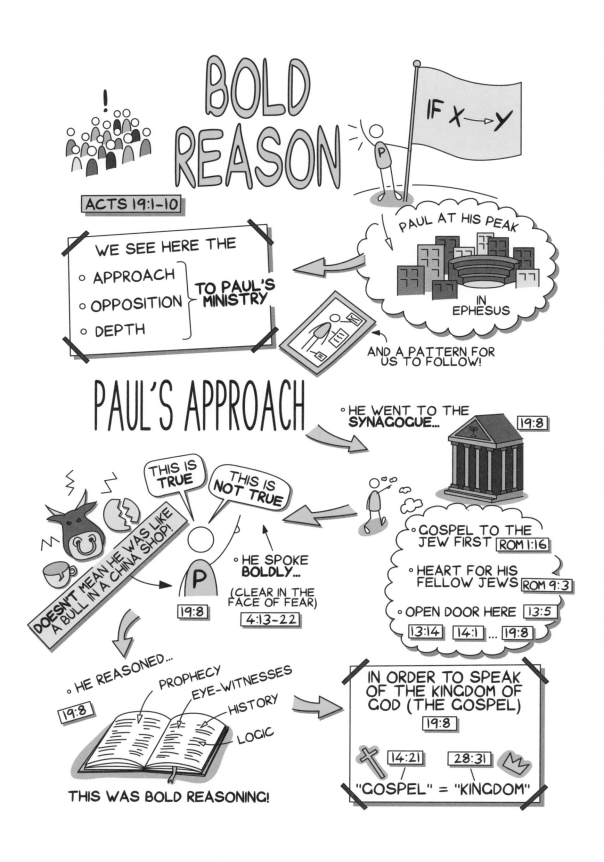

OPPOSITION TO PAUL'S MINISTRY 19:9

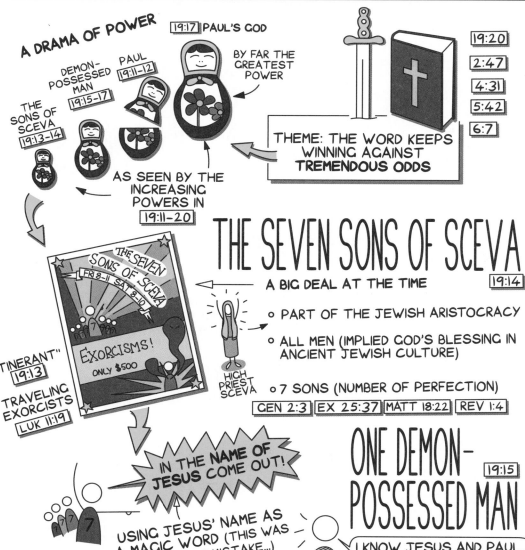

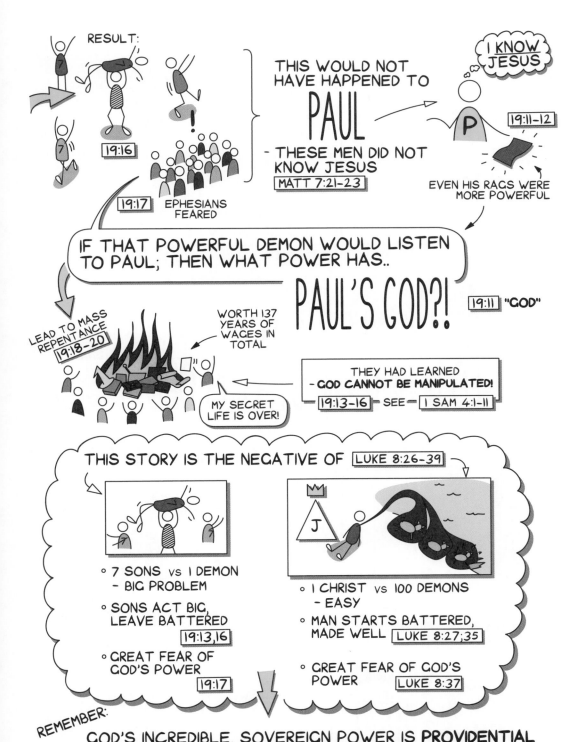

A GOSPEL RIOT

(IN EPHESUS)

ACTS 19:21-41

SUB-THEME IN ACTS

CHRISTIANS ARE REPEATEDLY VINDICATED FROM BEING CRIMINALS

ACTS 4:13-23; 5:33-41; 12:6-11; 16:35-39; 18:12-16; 26:10-12, 25; 26:30-32

CHRISTIANS MUST ALLOW THE GOSPEL TO UPSET THE STATUS QUO...

19:23-34

GOSPEL EFFECT

DEMETRIUS THE IDOL MAKER

19:24

- OUR BUSINESS WILL FALL INTO DISREPUTE! 19:25
- THE **TEMPLE** OF ARTEMIS (AND) EPHESUS WILL BE IGNORED! 19:27
- **ARTEMIS** WILL BE DEPOSED! 19:27

AAARGH!! 19:28

WHY ARE WE YELLING? 19:32

GREAT IS ARTEMIS OF THE EPHESIANS!

(FOR 2 HOURS) 19:34

WHY SO MAD? ARTEMIS WAS THEIR **LIFE**

PEOPLE FOR SCALE

TEMPLE OF ARTEMIS

2.5 X LONGER THAN THE **WHITE HOUSE**!

THEY EQUATE ALEXANDER (A JEW) WITH PAUL (A JEW)

PAUL'S COMPANIONS DRAGGED IN 19:29

19:30-31
DON'T GO AND HELP, PAUL. IT'S TOO DANGEROUS

CONSIDER: MANY BUSINESSES WILL NOT LIKE CHRISTIANS CHANGING CULTURE

CONSUME! BUY! SALE!

ARE YOU ACTUALLY KEEPING SOME OF THESE PLACES OPEN?

...BUT WE MUST NOT BECOME RABBLE ROUSERS!

TOWN CLERK

ARTEMIS IS GREAT 19:35 BUT THESE MEN HAVE DONE **NOTHING WRONG!** 19:37-39

"SACRED STONE" 19:35 (COULD BE A METEORITE)

BUT ROME MAY PUNISH US FOR RIOTING! 19:40

CROWDS DISMISSED

WE SHOULD BE THANKFUL FOR GOOD LAWS

HOW DO WE WALK THIS TIGHTROPE?

QUESTIONS FOR CHRISTIAN RABBLE ROUSERS

ARE YOU CAREFUL TO KEEP LAWS WHICH DON'T REQUIRE YOU TO SIN?

DO YOU INTEND FOR YOUR WORDS AND ACTIONS TO BE MISUNDERSTOOD?

DO PEOPLE SEE YOU AS A HAPPY WARRIOR OR AN ANGRY MERCENARY?

QUESTIONS FOR CHRISTIANS AFRAID TO OFFEND

DO YOU REFUSE TO BE GODLY JUST BECAUSE IT WOULD LOOK STRANGE TO OTHERS?

IS YOUR LIFE A THREAT TO SINFUL PRACTICES AND THOSE LIVING BY THEM?

DO YOU FEAR OPINION MORE THAN GOD?

TO SURVIVE AS A CHRISTIAN, WE MUST **DIE** TO THE APPROVAL OF OTHERS

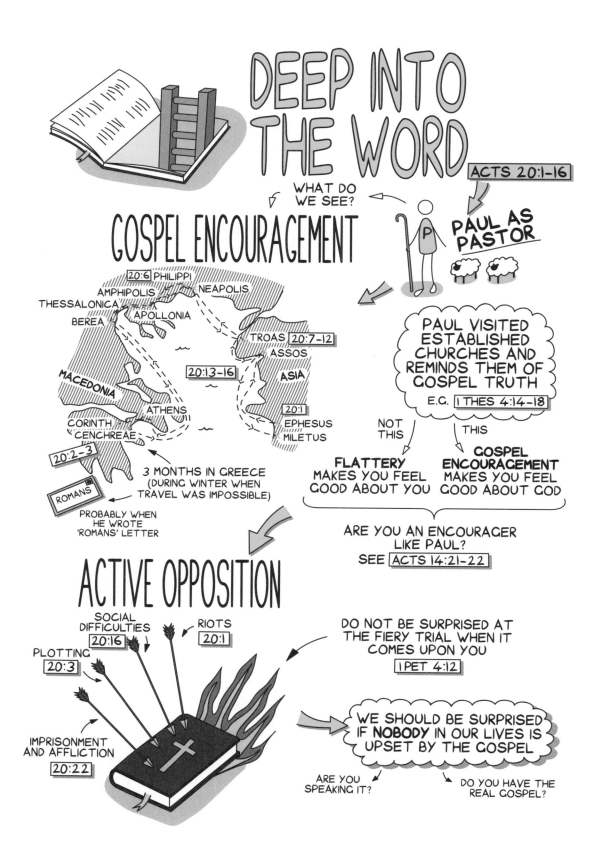

PAUL SETS THE PRIORITIES

ACTS 20:17-38

THESE ARE THE PRIORITIES FOR...

HOW DO WE MAKE SURE WE FINISH THE RACE WELL?

2 TIM 4:7

FINISH

20:24

PAUL

20:18-21 (SEE THE WORD-PAIRS)

HOW?	WHAT?	WHERE?	TO WHO?	SAYING?
WITH "HUMILITY" AND "TEARS"	"DECLARING" AND "TEACHING"	IN "PUBLIC" AND "HOUSES"	"JEWS" AND "GENTILES"	"REPENTANCE" AND "FAITH"
20:19	20:20	20:20	20:21	20:21

THESE SHOULD BE THE PRIORITIES OF THE CHURCH

FOR... **PASTORS**

① DO NOT SHRINK FROM **SUFFERING**

I MUST GO TO JERUSALEM- DESPITE THE THREATS

20:22-23

DEATH 20:23-25

PAUL VALUED THE MESSAGE OF THE CROSS MORE THAN HE FEARED CARRYING HIS CROSS

IF A PASTOR VALUES HIS LIFE OVER THE GOSPEL, THE CHURCH WILL SUFFER

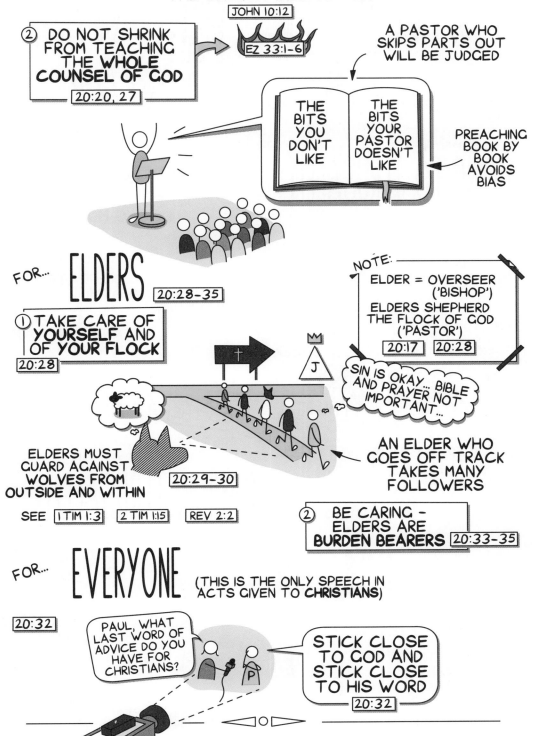

WHEN THE HARD WAY IS THE BEST WAY

ACTS 21:1-26

GOING TO JERUSALEM

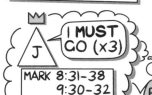

COS
RHODES
PATARA
CYPRUS
21:1
21:4
21:7-8
TYRE
PTOLEMAIS
CAESAREA
JERUSALEM

HOW DO YOU LIVE THE CHRISTIAN LIFE WHEN THE FUTURE LOOKS MURKY?

PROPHET AGABUS
21:10-11

REPEATED WARNING THAT GOING TO JERUSALEM MEANT CAPTURE AND DEATH

THE LAST LEG OF PAUL'S THIRD MISSIONARY TRIP

NO

I MUST GO (x3)

J

I MUST GO (x3)

P

21:12

PAUL DON'T GO THERE!

(JUST LIKE THEY SAID TO JESUS)

MARK 8:31-38
9:30-32
10:32-34

20:22   21:4
21:11

MATT 16:22

PAUL IN JERUSALEM

WITH GENTILES
P

THE JEWISH CHRISTIANS HERE THINK YOU TELL PEOPLE THAT THEY CANNOT KEEP JEWISH RITUAL LAWS!
21:19-22

SO WE SUGGEST...

HMM... SO HE IS OK WITH JEWISH CUSTOMS!

P

JOIN THESE JEWISH MEN IN A VOW

RESULT
21:24

21:23-24

...FOR THE SAKE OF THE GOSPEL BEING HEARD!

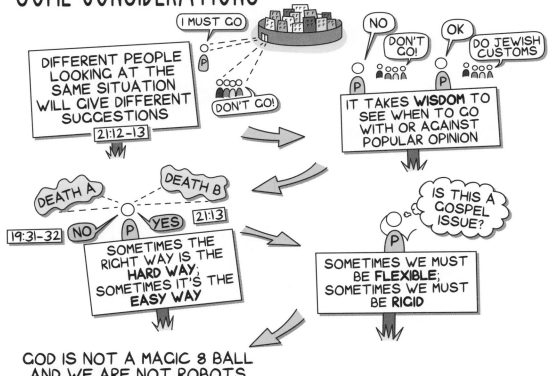

ARREST, RIOT, DEFENSE

ACTS 21:17-22:21

ACTS CONTENTS

1-7 JERUSALEM & DISCIPLES

8-12 JUDEA, SAMARIA, PETER

13-21 PAUL'S MISSIONS

21-28 **PAUL AS PRISONER**

THIS IS **PAUL AS APOLOGIST**

IN JERUSALEM

HE MAKES 5 DEFENSES

○ THE MOB IN JERUSALEM 22:1-21
○ THE COUNCIL 23:1-22
○ FELIX THE GOVERNOR 24:10-21
○ FESTUS THE GOVERNOR 25:1-12
○ AGRIPPA THE KING 26:1-29

ʾΑπολογία 'APOLOGIA' A DEFENSE (E.G 22:1)

PAUL HAD REASON TO GIVE A DEFENSE

SERIOUS THEOLOGICAL DISAGREEMENT

○ WHO WAS JESUS?
○ ROLE OF THE TEMPLE?
○ JEWISH CUSTOMS?
○ FAITH VS WORKS?

NO GENTILE ZONE

MISINFORMATION
PAUL BROUGHT GENTILES INTO THE TEMPLE! 21:28
(LUKE CORRECTS) 21:29

ROME SENT ABOUT 200 MEN TO GET PAUL AND DISPEL THE RIOT 21:30-36

HATRED OF PAUL
THAT'S THE GUY WHO TURNED OUR CITY UPSIDE DOWN! 17:6

NOTE: THESE JEWS ARE FROM **ASIA**, NOT JERUSALEM!

GET HIM!

ANTI-JEW 21:28
ANTI-LAW
ANTI-TEMPLE

PAUL HAS BEEN **LABELLED**

THE COURAGE TO BEAR WITNESS

ACTS 22:22-23:11

(PAUL'S 2ND DEFENSE)

PAUL BEFORE THE TRIBUNE
22:22-29

PAUL BEFORE THE COUNCIL
22:30-23:10

WE LEARN 3 SURPRISING LESSONS FROM PAUL AND 1 SURPRISING EXHORTATION FROM THE LORD

IT'S NOT WRONG TO ASSERT YOUR RIGHTS

22:22-29

AWAY WITH HIM!
JOHN 19:15

J →
JOHN 19:1

AWAY WITH HIM!
ACTS 22:22

SCOURGE WHIP

PIECES OF BONE

WHAT HAPPENED TO JESUS WAS HAPPENING TO PAUL
BUT...

BUT I AM A ROMAN CITIZEN!
22:24-29

TURN THE OTHER CHEEK

J
MATT 5:39-40

GIVE WHAT IS ASKED FROM YOU

JESUS WAS AGAINST **PERSONAL** RETALIATION

SO PAUL IS UNBOUND AND BROUGHT BEFORE THE COUNCIL
22:30

'TO FLOG A ROMAN CITIZEN IS AN ABOMINATION' CICERO, ROMAN CONSUL 63BC

HOWEVER

PAUL ASSERTS HIS RIGHTS FOR THE **SAKE OF THE GOSPEL**

IT'S NOT WRONG TO ADMIT YOU ARE WRONG

P — BROTHERS, I HAVE DONE NO WRONG! `23:1`

`23:2`

GOD WILL STRIKE YOU, YOU EMPTY FAKE! `23:3`

WRONG TO SPEAK LIKE THIS TO HIS ELDER... `EX 22:28`

SORRY `23:5`

...AS PAUL IMMEDIATELY ACKNOWLEDGES

IT'S NOT WRONG TO BE SHREWD

SADDUCEES **DID NOT** BELIEVE IN THE RESURRECTION

`23:6`

PHARISEES **DID** BELIEVE IN THE RESURRECTION

PAUL DIVIDED THE ENEMY `23:7-8`

I AM A **PHARISEE** AND I BELIEVE IN THE **RESURRECTION!**

PHARISEES STAND UP FOR THEIR FELLOW PHARISEE, PAUL `23:9`

WE ARE TO BE **WISE AS SERPENTS** AND **INNOCENT AS DOVES**

AN UNSURPRISING EXHORTATION FROM GOD

TAKE **COURAGE**, YOU MUST TESTIFY IN ROME

`23:11` **J** **P**

IN OUR EVERYDAY OPPORTUNITIES TO SPEAK THE GOSPEL, GOD STANDS WITH US SO WE NEED NOT BE AFRAID

`23:11` `PS 56:3-4` `2 TIM 4:16-18`

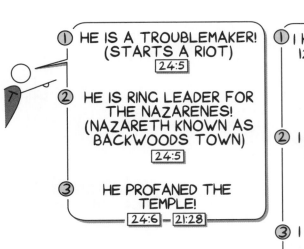

① HE IS A TROUBLEMAKER! (STARTS A RIOT) `24:5`

② HE IS RING LEADER FOR THE NAZARENES! (NAZARETH KNOWN AS BACKWOODS TOWN) `24:5`

③ HE PROFANED THE TEMPLE! `24:6` – `21:28`

① I HAVE BEEN BACK FOR 12 DAYS – THEY HAVE NOT SEEN ME CAUSING RIOTS! `24:11-13`

② I BELIEVE IN THE SAME SCRIPTURE, GOD AND RESURRECTION AS THEM! `24:14-15`

③ I BROUGHT OFFERINGS TO THE TEMPLE! `24:16-17`

AND WHERE ARE THE JEWS FROM ASIA WHO WISH TO CHARGE ME? **NOT HERE!**

◁ **SOLID DEFENSE**

BUT PAUL IS ON TRIAL CONCERNING...

THE RESURRECTION OF THE DEAD `24:21`

IF JESUS HAS BEEN RAISED FROM THE DEAD... ➡

THEN THIS WAS A MATTER OF THEOLOGY; NOT LAW

➡ THEN THE SADDUCEES WERE **WRONG**

➡ PAUL WAS A LEADER OF GOD'S PEOPLE

THEN HE WAS NOT THE FOUNDER OF A SECT, BUT THE **CHRIST**

`2:24` `3:15` `4:10`
`4:12` `13:30` `17:3`

KING `PS 2`

HOLY ONE `PS 16`

LORD `PS 110`

THEN THE RESURRECTION OF ALL PEOPLE... `DAN 12:2`

...IS **SECURED** BY CHRIST'S RESURRECTION `ACTS 4:2` → "IN JESUS"

WAS JESUS RAISED? IF SO, THIS CHANGES **EVERYTHING**

FAITH HAS ITS REASONS

ACTS 24:22-27

DIFFERENT PLACE, SAME PASSION

PAUL HELD IN PRISON
INDEFINITELY

- NOTE THE NEED FOR
OUTSIDE HELP IN
ROMAN PRISONS
24:23   2 TIM 4:9-13

NO MATTER WHERE HE WAS...

JESUS	JESUS	JESUS	JESUS	JESUS
17:1-2	17:17	17:30-31	22:8	24:24

...PAUL'S PASSION REMAINED

WHAT TOPIC DO YOUR
CONVERSATIONS ALWAYS COME
BACK TO?

CHRIST IS THE ONLY PASSION
WHICH WILL NEVER DISAPPOINT

LUKE 12:22-31   DEUT 31:6

DIFFERENT APPROACH, SAME GOSPEL

WHEN TO DIE WHEN TO TRY

ACTS 25:1-27 (PAUL'S 4TH DEFENSE)

JERUSALEM

WE STILL WANT PAUL DEAD!

25:1-5

AS THIS PASSAGE SHOWS, SOMETIMES LIFE SEEMS TOTALLY UNFAIR

2 YEARS LATER... 24:27

YOU MAY ACCUSE HIM AT CAESAREA

GOVERNOR FESTUS

25:6-7

I HAVE DONE NOTHING AGAINST

○ THE JEWS
○ THE TEMPLE
○ ROME 25:8

○ THIS MAN IS INNOCENT 25:10 25:25
○ THIS IS A THEOLOGICAL MATTER 25:19

IF I HAVE DONE WRONG THEN PUNISH ME! 25:11

TAKE ME TO ROME! 25:11-12

PAUL'S UNWORTHY JUDGES

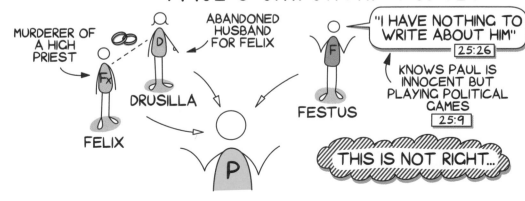

MURDERER OF A HIGH PRIEST

ABANDONED HUSBAND FOR FELIX

"I HAVE NOTHING TO WRITE ABOUT HIM" 25:26

KNOWS PAUL IS INNOCENT BUT PLAYING POLITICAL GAMES 25:9

DRUSILLA

FELIX

FESTUS

THIS IS NOT RIGHT...

WHY IS IT THOUGHT INCREDIBLE THAT GOD RAISES THE DEAD?

(PAUL'S 5TH DEFENSE)

ACTS 26:1-11

BERNICE

KING AGRIPPA WELL VERSED IN JEWISH CUSTOMS
26:2-3

APART FROM THE RESURRECTION

...YOU CANNOT UNDERSTAND THESE CONTROVERSIES...

26:4-8

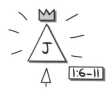

1:6-11

THE WHOLE CHRISTIAN RELIGION PIVOTS ON WHETHER JESUS CHRIST IS **DEAD** OR **ALIVE**

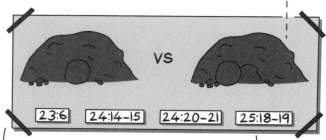

VS

23:6   24:14-15   24:20-21   25:18-19

IF **DEAD** CHRISTIANITY IS **WORTHLESS** AND CHRISTIANS ARE TO BE PITIED
1 COR 15:12-19

IF **ALIVE**, EVERY ASPECT OF LIFE CHANGES
26:12-23

ACTS 7

I AM SIMPLY A JEW WHO HAS **SEEN** THESE PROMISES FULFILLED!
26:4-7; 22-23

BUILT ON 2 FACTS
- JESUS' EMPTY TOMB
- JESUS APPEARED TO MANY AFTER HE ROSE | 1 COR 15:3-8 |

WORLD RELIGIONS RELY UPON PRIVATE MESSAGES FROM GOD...

CHRISTIANITY RELIES UPON PUBLIC EVENTS

...YOU CANNOT UNDERSTAND ME | 26:9-11 |

I WAS A FUNDAMENTALIST JEW! | 26:4,5 |

NOBODY HATED CHRISTIANS AS MUCH AS I DID!

| DEATH | LIFE | BALLOT | 26:10 |

BLASPHEME! | 26:11 |

BUT NOW I AM ON TRIAL FOR HAVING **HOPE IN GOD'S PROMISES** | 26:6 |

| DAN 12:2 |

| IS 25:8; 26:19 | | EZ 37:13 |

IF YOU ARE A CHRISTIAN

DOES YOUR LIFE MAKE SENSE WITHOUT THE RESURRECTION?
(IT SHOULDN'T)

IF YOU ARE NOT A CHRISTIAN

WHY DO YOU THINK IT'S INCREDIBLE THAT GOD RAISES THE DEAD?
(IT ISN'T)

◁○▷

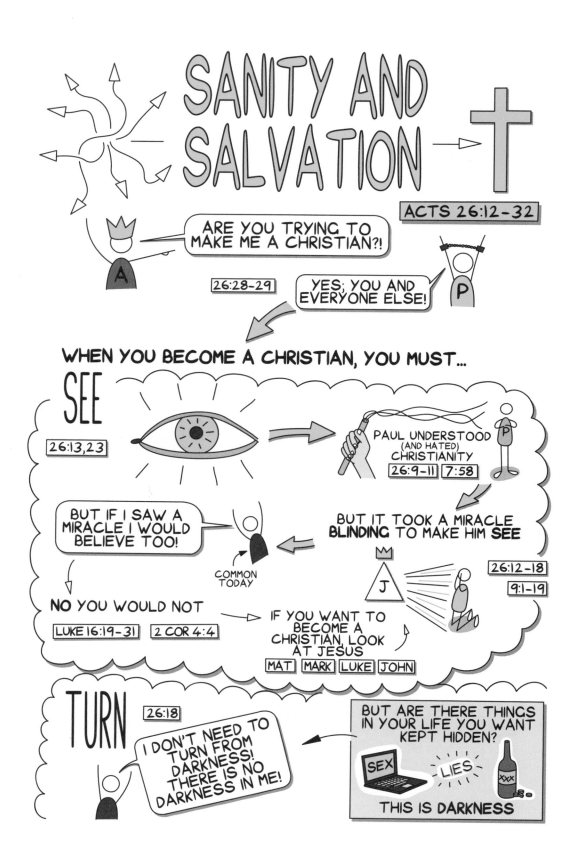

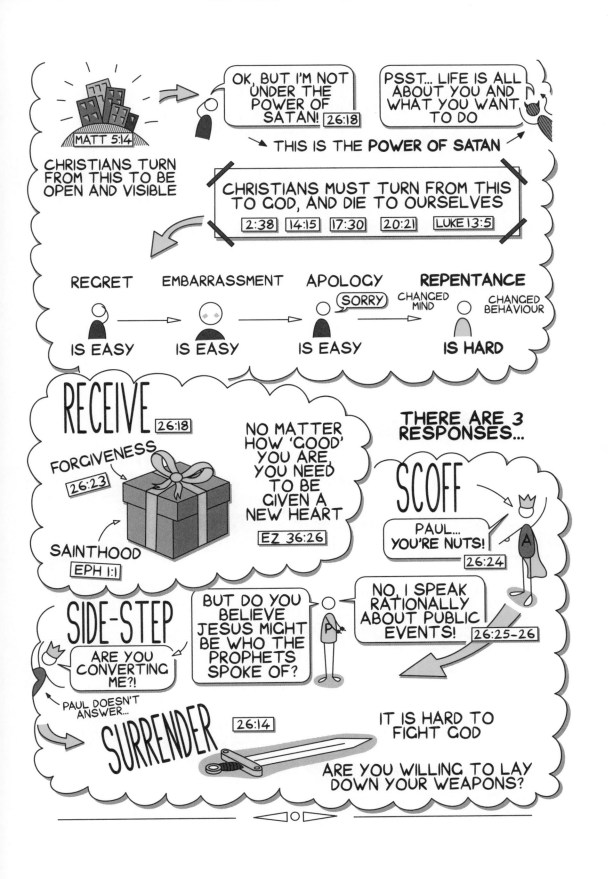

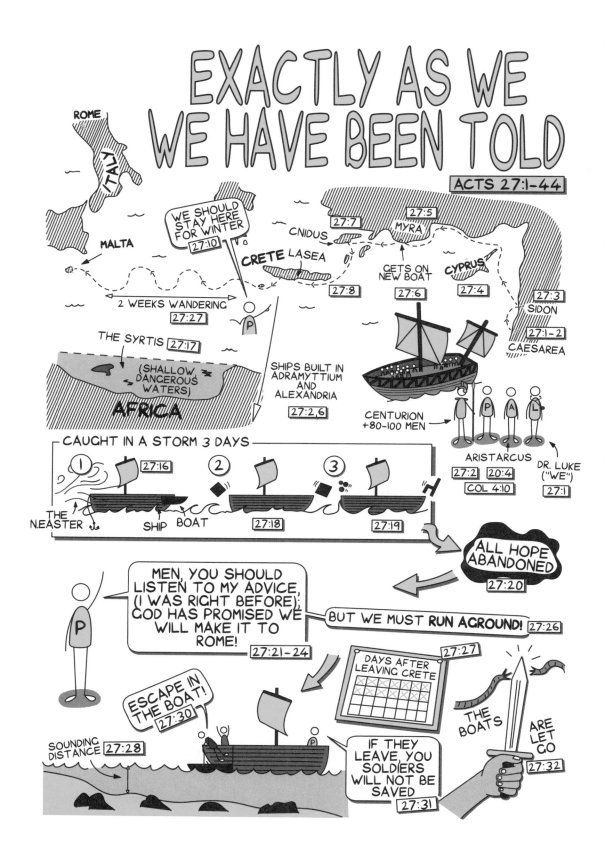

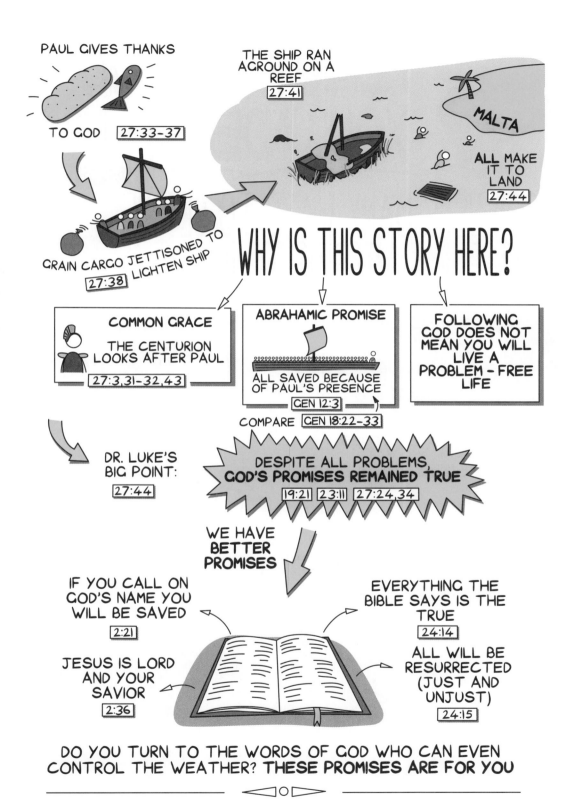

HEARING, BUT DO YOU UNDERSTAND?

ACTS 28:1-28

GOD USES MANY WAYS TO GET US WHERE HE WANTS US TO BE...

ON MALTA...

PAUL MEETS THE NATIVES (NON-GREEK SPEAKERS)
28:1-2

28:3

- DEATH → PAUL WAS A CRIMINAL 28:4 (‘JUSTICE’ = ‘GOD’) IF
- NO HARM → PAUL WAS A GOD 28:6 IF

NOTE: NO SHARED LANGUAGE SO NO OBVIOUS GOSPEL MESSAGE SPOKEN

ALTHOUGH PAUL HEALED MANY OVER THE WINTER ON MALTA 28:7-10

ROME 28:14-16
THREE TAVERNS
APPII FORUM
PUTEOLI
28:13
RHEGIUM
SYRACUSE 28:12
28:11 MALTA

PAUL EVENTUALLY MAKES IT TO...
19:21 23:11 27:24

ROME

WHY WAS THIS SO IMPORTANT?

① PAUL WANTED TO BE VINDICATED

② THE GOSPEL NEEDED TO BE VINDICATED

③ GOD WANTED HIM TO TESTIFY THERE

BUT IF PAUL WANTED TO GO TO ROME AND GOD WANTED TO GO TO ROME - WHY WAS IT SO DIFFICULT TO GET THERE?

PRISON   DEFENSES   RIOTS   SHIPWRECK   PAIN

POSSIBLE REASONS

GOD WANTED TO SAVE PEOPLE

GOD WANTED PEOPLE TO PRAY FOR PAUL

REMINDER THAT PAUL WAS NOT IN CHARGE - GOD WAS

PAUL PREACHED TO MANY PEOPLE THROUGH ALL THIS
DO YOU VIEW YOUR DIFFICULTIES AS OPPORTUNITIES TO TELL PEOPLE ABOUT JESUS?

...GOD USES ONLY ONE MESSAGE TO SAVE FROM SIN

THIS IS WHY I APPEALED TO CAESAR... FOR THE HOPE IN THE RESURRECTION
28:17-20

EXTENDED TEACHING
28:23-24

OK WE SHALL HEAR YOU ABOUT THIS...
28:21-22

IN CONCLUSION... GOD WAS RIGHT WHEN HE SAID YOU WOULD **HEAR** BUT NOT **UNDERSTAND!**
28:25-27   IS 6:10

SO I WILL GO TO THE **GENTILES**
28:28

THIS IS A WARNING TO US TOO!

YOU CAN HEAR THE MESSAGE ALL YOU WANT ...

BUT YOU ARE ONLY UNDERSTANDING IF YOU KNOW 2 THINGS
YOU ARE A SINNER (PERSONALLY)
JESUS IS YOUR SAVIOR (PERSONALLY)

BOLDLY AND WITHOUT HINDRANCE

ACTS 28:30-31

AN ABRUPT ENDING TO ACTS

WHAT?!

WHAT HAPPENED TO PAUL?!

THE END!

BUT AN APPROPRIATE ENDING FOR...

THE LAST SECTION OF THE BOOK

THE GOSPEL MUST GO TO ROME!

19:21 23:11 27:24

THE WHOLE BOOK

THE GOSPEL WILL GO TO THE ENDS OF THE EARTH!

1:8

MISSION ACCOMPLISHED

WHAT HAVE WE LEARNED?

THE MISSION OF THE CHURCH IS THE MESSAGE OF THE GOSPEL

- DIED AND ROSE
- FULFILLMENT OF PROPHECY
- KINGDOM OF GOD

SEE ALSO LUKE 1:32-33

1:1-3

28:28-31

'INCLUSIO' (START MATCHES END TO MAKE A POINT)

- JESUS DIED AND ROSE
- HE FULFILLED PROPHECY
- KINGDOM OF GOD

PAUL SPOKE **BOLDLY**

28:31

DO YOU?

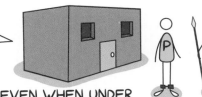

EVEN WHEN UNDER
HOUSE ARREST

WILL YOU
MEET HIS
GUARD
ONE DAY?

28:16

THE MOST IMPORTANT STORY IS THE GOSPEL STORY

IT IS THE STORY OF HOW
CHRIST REACHED THE
NATIONS WITH HIS WORD

ACTS IS NOT A
BIOGRAPHY OF
PETER, PAUL OR THE
EARLY CHURCH

LUKE'S POINT IS NOT THAT PAUL WOULD ONE DAY DIE
BUT THAT **THE GOSPEL WILL ALWAYS LIVE**

THE GOSPEL WILL BE THREATENED BUT NEVER SILENCED

6:7 9:31 12:24 16:5 19:20

BUT THE
GOSPEL IS
"UNHINDERED"

THE GOSPEL ALWAYS
INCREASED, DESPITE
MANY SETBACKS

PAUL MIGHT BE
IMPRISONED

THE LAST WORD IN ACTS

SO, LIKE THE EARLY CHURCH, BELIEVE THAT
THE WORD OF GOD
IS SUFFICIENT TO DO THE WORK OF GOD

◄─◐─►

VISUALISING SERMONS

We have all been there... it's 11.30 on a Sunday morning and the preacher is finishing up on point two of a three point sermon. Looking down, your open notebook resembles a white cat in a snowstorm and your mind has once again drifted off to other things. This was my experience for many years until I started to draw what the preacher was saying.

This technique, known as Visual Note-Taking, can help anyone to stay focused during sermons and makes revision of the message far more effective. With ordinary notes it is possible to make the mistake of simply writing out what the preacher is saying without thinking about the underlying message. But with visual notes, the note-taker has to first listen and understand what idea is being conveyed before spoken words can be transformed into a drawing—it is impossible to make visual notes that have bypassed your brain!

What's more, it's not just for the arty types. If you can draw a stick man, and you want to engage your brain in what you hear on a Sunday, then why not try taking visual notes for yourself? All you need is a pen, paper and the willingness to try something new (and fun).

Chris Ranson